# $\mathfrak{S}$uccess!
## with the
## Violin and Life

Strategies, Techniques & Tips
for Learning Quickly and Doing Well

# RUTH SHILLING

*Violin Success Series: 1*

All One World Books & Media

Cover design: Ruth Shilling

The violin watercolor on the cover was painted by Jennifer Chudy at age 11. She gave it to Ruth in 1996 and it still hangs in Ruth's teaching studio. Jennifer studied violin with Ruth for five years.

Jennifer Chudy & Ruth

Other illustrations: Ruth Shilling

Also by Ruth Shilling:

· Playing the Violin & Viola with Vibrato (ebook).

· TONE: Violin & Viola Bowing Techniques for a Rich, Satisfying Sound (ebook).

· SINAI: The Desert & Bedouins of South Sinai's Central Regions. Published by Palm Press, Cairo, Egypt, 2003. ISBN 978-9-7750895-2-6

Copyright © 2016 by Ruth Shilling
All rights reserved.

Published by All One World Books & Media, West Kingston, RI, USA
all1world.com

Library of Congress Control Number: 2016901296

Shilling, Ruth
    Success with the Violin and Life: Strategies, Techniques and Tips for Learning Quickly and Doing Well / Ruth Shilling. – 1st ed.
    Violin Success Series: 1.
    Includes index.
    MT259-338

ISBN : 978-0-9971991-0-9

PRINTED IN THE UNITED STATES OF AMERICA

This book is dedicated with gratitude

to the violin and viola teachers who have generously

shared their music and expertise with me.

Vincent Monicelli

Arnold Clair

John Dempsey

Jerome Lipson

Eberhard Klemmstein

Theodore Arm

Peter Sacco

Carol Glenn

I especially thank Eberhard Klemmstein.

Much of what is included in this book comes from

the five years I was under his tutelage.

✳ ✳ ✳ ✳ ✳ ✳ ✳ ✳ ✳ ✳ ✳

# Table of Contents

◆◆◆◆◆◆◆◆◆◆◆◆◆◆◆◆◆◆◆◆◆◆◆◆◆◆◆◆◆◆◆

# LIST OF STORIES

◆◆◆◆◆◆◆◆◆◆◆◆◆◆◆◆◆◆◆◆◆◆◆◆◆◆◆◆◆◆◆◆◆◆◆

# Introduction

### Story: First Violin Lesson

One day a fellow violin teacher told me she had just given a young boy his first violin lesson. She started off the lesson showing him how to hold the bow, the violin, and the first rhythms he would play.

As the lesson progressed, he began getting impatient, and asked her to show him how she played the violin. After she played something for him, he asked, "How do you do it?"

She explained to him, that what she was showing him with the bow hold, etc. was so that he would be able to play that way, too.

"But how do you do it?" he asked again. They kept going back and forth, with him asking how she did it, and her trying to explain that it was a *process*, something you learn in steps...

Then he tried a different tactic. He came very close to her and whispered, "But what's the secret?"

Explaining that there wasn't any secret didn't fly.

Now enraged, he yelled, "You know, AND YOU JUST WON'T TELL ME!"

To that she answered, "The secret is PRACTICE."

### *From the boy's perspective*

Although this story may seem amusing to us, imagine how it was from the boy's perspective. Up until that point, learning how to do things was pretty straight forward. To make the light go on, flip the switch. To turn on the TV, press a button. To make the letter "B," you do it like this. That's how we learn to do things, right?

### *Not like flipping a switch*

Developing a skill is a different story. It evolves through sustained focus and efforts over time, and includes lots of repetition!

### *Growth spurts & plateaus*

Sometimes we see marvelous results with very little effort and other times we just plug away like putting one more penny into the piggy bank, hoping someday it will add up to a dollar. If we keep at it, we will have good days, lousy days, plateaus and growth spurts. All are natural parts of the journey when learning a skill.

### *But, there ARE some incredibly helpful "secrets"!*

The good news contained in the pages of this book is that there are "secrets" that can speed up your learning process considerably!

Learning skills can be much, much easier and faster if a person knows and applies some universal success principles. An example is the way Bernie had spent many days trying to improve his speed on a passage without much result, but in his lesson was able to increase his speed by five metronome markings in just 15 minutes (pages 45-48). You can look forward to results like that, too!

### As on the violin, so with other life skills

While the principles explained here will greatly facilitate your progress on the violin, they are universal (not just specific to violin playing), so can be applied to other areas of life as well. People may think of it as being "multitalented," but actually, once we have learned the *process* of attaining skills, we can easily apply that to other things we do.

### Violin *(also Viola, Cello and Bass)*

The first section of each chapter gives specific applications to playing the violin (as well as other stringed instruments) – step-by-step applications, strategies, and techniques, as well as lots of helpful tips about playing and performing.

### Life

The second section of each chapter gives ways to apply those same concepts and principles to other aspects of life.

*I hope you enjoy it and find it fruitful.*

*To your SUCCESS!*

*– Ruth Shilling*

CHAPTER ONE

# Practice Being Successful

Skills cannot be bought or given away. We acquire them through our own actions over time. But good guidance and the knowledge of *how to most easily acquire a skill* makes a huge difference. Applying some universal principles for successful achievement can save us vast amounts of time and effort!

Many highly competent people at the top of their fields, including the majority of entrepreneurs, learned to play an instrument when they were young. They invested time and effort in hours of practice, they got a taste for the momentum brought by inspired action and focused desire, and they delighted in the sweet satisfaction of accomplishment.

A man, who made a profession of showing others how to achieve skills in the shortest amount of time, demonstrated one of his strategies in a dramatic way.

## Story: Success Breeds Success

John* had never fired a gun in his life and knew nothing about target shooting. He went to a shooting club and asked how long it usually took to achieve a certain level of success. The answer was about 2-3 months.

John first needed to learn how to shoot a pistol. When he fired it the first time there was a kick back and all the guys were laughing at his reaction.

The next thing he did was to walk all the way up to the target, stick the gun right on the bullseye and fire. SUCCESS! Bullseye!

The guys standing around were not impressed. Of course he could get a bullseye if he stuck the gun right on it.

What John then began to do was to gradually move away from the target, constantly shooting directly into the bullseye and each time feeling the satisfaction of achieving his goal.

So his pattern was:
**Success, Rejoice, Satisfaction.**

And what was the result? Within *just two weeks* he was shooting at a level that would normally take 2-3 *months*.

---

*All of the stories in this book are from the author's own personal experiences, however, many of the names used in the stories have been changed.

## Practicing Being Successful vs. Using Willpower to Continue While Failing

Why does repeatedly being successful yield better and faster results than trying again and again, despite failing, until you finally get it?

Let's look at the target shooting example.

John's goal may have been to shoot a bullseye at 30 feet. He could have started standing 30 feet away and shooting. Each time he would have failed, but he may have gotten closer and closer with repeated attempts. If he had the willpower to keep trying despite his constant defeats, he would probably eventually be able to achieve his goal. But during that process he would be constantly dealing with defeat.

People who work to achieve skills learn to deal with defeat and keep going, but getting back up on the horse after falling takes effort. It is hard on the ego to fail and we have to use willpower to override feeling deflated by it. Having willpower is good, but constantly dealing with defeat is like pushing uphill rather than coasting downhill.

John, on the other hand, chose to constantly experience being successful. That feeling of "Hurray!" was like the wind at his back. It provided a momentum that naturally wanted to carry him forward.

## Body memory imprint

Another aspect of working with repeated success, as opposed to repeated failures, is that the body learns by doing. If the body does something well or not well, either way it is establishing a sort of groove, like a rut in a field where people keep driving the same route.

Our bodies remember the way it was done before and are most likely to do it in a similar way the next time. It will always be easier to do it that way, rather than a different way.

So if you fail the first time, the next time you attempt to do it your body will most likely do it in a similar way, which will mean failing again.

If on the other hand, you experience success the first time you try to do something, that makes an imprint in your body memory which will make it more likely that next time you will also be successful.

## Imprint of connection

In the target shooting example John's body, mind and spirit were repeatedly making a connection with the bullseye. This *imprint of connection* guided him towards replicating that success as he challenged himself to achieve the more difficult goal of moving farther away from the target.

## Visualizing success

Another aspect which contributes to this is *the ability to visualize success*. Athletes and high achievers are well aware of how the power of visualizing helps them to accomplish their goals. Having a series of successful experiences to draw on helps us to recreate them in our mind's eye. It is a lot easier to visualize success when we have already experienced it!

### Where does willpower come in?

Willpower always has an important role in learning skills. Without it we would be unfocused and our attempts to achieve things would be short-lived. Even when we are working with the success model, we will have defeats. We will still need to "get back on the horse" when we don't achieve our goals.

### What about aiming high?

When we build from success to success, we are aiming high, but doing it in steps. However, sometimes taking a chance at a big leap forward without doing the groundwork is worthwhile, too, and can be exhilarating. Even if a goal appears unobtainable right now, it is still worth having the courage to give it a shot. We might be lucky and hit it! So that is part of the process of going beyond our limitations, too. However, if we do this repeatedly and fail at hitting the goal, we lose ground and have to make it up again by doing additional careful stepwise work.

### "Practicing is making SUCCESS a habit."

Since 1988 there has been a sign in my studio that says "Practicing is making SUCCESS a habit." That concept can be easy to forget, but my students certainly hear it a lot!

## REPEATEDLY DOING SOMETHING WELL
### *The Best Use of Your Practice Time*

*Example:*

## IMPROVING YOUR INTONATION
If you want to improve your intonation on a particular passage, figure out a way that you *can* play the notes in tune.

Devise a method that will enable you to play each note correctly, and then repeat that until it becomes reliable.

*Suggestions of methods to try:*

### 1. Slower
Could you play each note in tune if you played it slowly?

### 2. Stop-Prepare
Can you get it right if you use *Stop-Prepare* (pause between the notes and then consciously choose where to place your next finger)? It is best to do *Stop-Prepare* with an intentional rhythm, so use the metronome. Add a one or two beat rest for the time you need to stop and prepare the next note.

### 3. Tuner, open strings
Would it help to use an electronic tuner to find out where those notes are on the fingerboard? Can you check with any open strings to see if the note is right?

## 4. Finger spacings

Note the finger spacings from one note to the next. How close are they to the other fingers? Be sure you know the distance between them. Notice how your fingers feel when they are in the right place on the fingerboard, and how they feel when they are in the right relationship to each other. Memorize that feeling.

## 5. Hear it before playing it

Can you hear what each note should be *before* you play it? Can you sing the intervals? Playing the passage on the piano first can help you to know what it should sound like. Sing what you think the next note is before playing it on the piano.

## 6. Play with the piano

If you have someone who can play the passage on the piano while you play it on the violin, doing that could help a lot. Having the piano play an octave lower is usually better than in unison. If you have a digital recorder, you can play it on the piano yourself and then play the violin with the recording. Some keyboards will also record it and play it back.

## 7. Make all the notes the same length

Play every note as a quarter note, rather than the rhythm as it occurs in the piece. That way you will be able to focus totally on the finger placements. Play with a solid, healthy, loud tone so you hear it clearly.

## 8. Double stops

If the notes are on two strings, play them as double stops and remember the way your fingers feel in relation to each other as well as your hand position.

As you are practicing in those ways, remember to:

### *Enjoy hitting it right on.*

Feel the satisfaction you get from the vibration and resonance the instrument gives you when the note is just right.

### *Repeat until it is easy and solid.*

Once you find a way that you can get the note(s) in tune, do it repeatedly until it feels **easy and reliable**. Once you can do it easily, play it at least 5-10 more times *in a row without mistakes*. Memorize that experience and the feeling of security you now have as you play it.

### *Yes!*

Enjoy the feeling of knowing that you can do it now. Have a "Yes!" feeling each time you play it in tune. Like the man who kept hitting the target, your pattern can be:

**Success, Rejoice, Satisfaction.**

◆◆◆◆◆◆◆◆◆◆◆◆◆◆◆◆◆◆◆◆◆◆◆◆◆◆◆◆◆◆◆

# Building from Success to Success in Life

## *Story: One Success Builds to Greater Successes*

I once met a man in his mid-twenties who already owned and operated a very successful piano business. He did not even have a college degree, and yet he had a large number of employees, three of whom had PhD's. He had already gained an international reputation in piano sales, and he had made a lot of money, too!

How did this happen?

When Mark was about 14 years old, someone gave him an old upright piano that was in sorry need of some major repairs. He had a wonderful time tinkering with it and learning about how a piano works. Eventually, he got it fixed up and sold it. He was thrilled with his ability to do it and with the profit it brought him!

With the money from the sale of the piano, he bought a do-it-yourself kit with all the pieces needed to build a harpsichord. He built the harpsichord and sold that at a tidy profit as well.

That enabled him to buy another bigger and better kit . . . Within about ten years he owned two warehouses full of Bechstein grand pianos and a lucrative international business.

Mark's success was built by first being successful at a small goal and then building upward and outward from there. Success builds on success.

---

### Story: *"I can play every note in every piece of music."*

At the time that Mary Elizabeth Leach finished high school and applied to music school, the three top places to study music were the Julliard School, the New England Conservatory of Music, and the Curtis Institute. The chances of being admitted to one of these schools, especially as a pianist, were slim. To say that it was competitive would be an understatement.

Mary Elizabeth chose to apply to the New England Conservatory, and was not only accepted, but was one of the few piano majors to receive a nearly full-tuition scholarship (based on her skills).

Many years later she told me, "The most important breakthrough in my musical development came when I was in the 6th grade. It suddenly occurred to me that I had ten fingers, and I knew how to read and play every single note on the piano, so I could play virtually *any* piano piece in the world, provided I played it slowly enough!

"I got excited, and asked my father – who was a musician himself – what the most difficult piece of music was that we had in the house. He pulled it off the shelf for me. I was completely confident that I could learn it, and so I did, one note at a time.

"After that, nothing stopped me. I knew that I could play anything."

The piece she learned to play was Mendelssohn's *Rondo Capriccioso*. In the years to come, it became one of her signature pieces. In fact, it was one of the pieces she played for her audition at the conservatory.

How was she able to play such a difficult piece?

"At first I played each individual note so slowly that it was almost absurd, but even at that pace, I made sure to learn the notes in the correct rhythm. I practiced with a metronome. I went through the piece from beginning to end, over and over. Gradually, I turned up the speed on the metronome. After I became familiar with all of the notes, I practiced the more difficult sections individually."

> Building from
> one success to the next
> is a sure way to reach your goal
> and to have
> a tremendous amount of
> enjoyment and satisfaction
> along the way.

◆◆◆◆◆◆◆◆◆◆◆◆◆◆◆◆◆◆◆◆◆◆◆◆◆

# CHAPTER TWO

# Setting Goals

Clarifying our Goals is essential for using our time and energies effectively. Goals can be altered as we go along, but the shortest distance between two points will always be a straight line.

Clear goals help when choosing a violin method, a teacher, an instrument and new repertoire. Goals also focus us so that we get the maximum benefit out of our practice sessions.

## Departure and Arrival Points

When we plan a road trip, the two most important things to know are the departure and arrival points. "How do I get there from here?" When learning and playing the violin, thinking about where we are (how well we can play something now), and where we want to go, is just as worthwhile.

## When Changes are Needed

Keeping focused on the goal will guide us if we need to make midcourse changes to our route or strategy. As I embark on a road trip, I may need to adjust the route as unforeseen circumstances arise, but I still keep my destination in mind. Having a clear goal helps us to make wise choices when changes in our original plan are needed.

## Motivation to Persevere

Desiring a particular goal provides ongoing motivation to persevere, even when the going gets rough. The mountain climber or hiker wants to reach the summit. That desire keeps him going and pushing forward when he gets tired and might have called it quits. Likewise, if we really want to play a particular piece of music, that can motivate us to keep going even though it takes a long time to learn it.

## Story: "I want to play the Bach Double."

An 8-year old student named Jacob had been studying the violin for about one year when he watched a movie about a woman teaching violin using the Suzuki violin method. In the movie, a large group of children played the first movement of the J.S. Bach Violin Concerto for two violins. He just loved the piece and wanted to play it. His desire was on fire!

At his next lesson, he asked me if he could learn it. That piece is at the end of the Suzuki Book 4, and he was still just part way through Suzuki Book 1. It would have made sense to tell him that someday he would play that piece, but there were many other things he needed to learn first.

As I looked at him, I could feel how strong his desire was. I made the choice to see how much benefit we could get out of that desire.

"Well, you probably *could* play it, but it would take many, many hours of practice."

"How many?"

I told him something like 1,000 hours of practicing. He only paused a moment before he said he would do it. So we started that day to learn the first few measures.

Months later, he and I performed the piece on the student recital to much enthusiastic applause. It was a high-spirited, brilliant performance!

---

## TYPES OF GOALS

It is of great benefit when we are clear on each of the following types of goals.

### 1. OVERALL GOAL

See possibilities listed in the next section.

### 2. LONG TERM GOAL

*Example*: Being well prepared for an upcoming performance.

### 3. SHORT TERM GOAL

*Example*: Being able to play a passage at a certain tempo for your next lesson.

### 4. IMMEDIATE GOAL

*Example*: Achieving a target tempo in a practice session.

### OVERALL GOALS for Learning to Play the Violin

This list may help you clarify what your own personal goals are. Each one of these examples would mean emphasizing a different skill set when learning to play.

1. A 65-year old man just retired and always wanted to play the violin. What he would like most is to be able to play Mozart string quartets with other amateur players.

2. A 45-year old woman wants to learn to play the violin so that she can play in a local fiddle group.

3. A 12-year old boy wants to be one of the best players in his school orchestra and to be selected to play in a regional orchestra.

4. A young mother wants to learn to play well enough to help teach her young child using the Suzuki violin method.

5. A woman wants to be able to play Christmas carols and hymns, and to play duets with her children.

6. A teenager wants to play electric violin in a rock band with his friends.

7. A college student who played violin in elementary school wants to learn how to play pop and jazz, to improvise, and play backup harmonies in a band.

8. A singer-songwriter plays guitar but wants to add some violin or viola into her coffeehouse performances.

9. A young player aspires to have a career as a soloist.

10. An adult beginner aspires to play in the local community orchestra.

As you might imagine, each of these goals would involve a different skill set. A unique combination of skills, and therefore different strategies, would be needed to achieve the goals each of these people have.

♦♦♦♦♦♦♦♦♦♦♦♦♦♦♦♦♦♦♦♦♦♦♦♦♦♦♦♦♦♦♦♦♦♦♦♦

# Overall Goals in Life

Our overall goals in life go along with our values – our basic beliefs about what is good, right, acceptable, desired, and worthwhile.

When we do not check in with ourselves to remember what our basic values are, we can get way off course.

Taking some time periodically to re-evaluate what our values and core beliefs are, and how those are playing out in our daily lives, can be both surprising and sobering but is always worthwhile. Sometimes the death of someone we know can shock us into doing this spontaneously.

Illness, accidents and disasters, also have a way of putting things in perspective. As one person said, her illness showed her not to sweat the small stuff, and it is almost *all* small stuff.

---

### What is Most Important?
If you would like to clarify what you feel is most important in your life, here is one way to find that out.

### Question:
If you knew for sure that one year from today you would experience a fatal accident (no second chances, that's it), what would you want to do *before* that happened? How would you spend your remaining 364 days? What would you do during the next month, the next week, today, right now?

---

◆◆◆◆◆◆◆◆◆◆◆◆◆◆◆◆◆◆◆◆◆◆◆◆◆◆◆◆◆◆◆◆◆

# CHAPTER THREE

# Which Skill Sets Do You Need?

Each of the people listed in Chapter 2 had a different goal for learning to play the violin. The shortest and most efficient route to each of their destinations is going to be different.

**BASIC SKILLS, Common Goals**
Although the ultimate destination is different for each one, they will all need to learn the following basic skills:
- Holding the instrument
- Proper fingering and left-hand position
- A good bow hold and bow technique
- Executing different rhythms
- Discerning correct pitches, intonation

**OTHER IMPORTANT SKILLS. Which do you need?**
Other than the basic skills, there are quite a few other skills which are needed by the accomplished violinist. However, many of the people on the previous list are not aspiring to have a professional career. Knowing which of these skills are most important to you is very helpful and can guide you towards making good decisions as to how to use your practice time most wisely, which teacher and violin method are best for you, and which shorter-term goals would benefit you the most.

## Reading Music

It would be helpful for most everyone to be able to read music, but for some of the goals that were listed, reading music is not essential. People who learn by only listening can play solos, improvise and do backup harmonies. However, they cannot play in a chamber music group or in an orchestra.

## Bowing Techniques

There are certain types of bowing that are necessary for more advanced pieces of music, but not for playing simple melodies. Staccato, spiccato, portato, etc., will all be called for when playing music in the typical orchestral literature, as well as violin sonatas and chamber music.

Fiddle players will want to be good at rapid bow crossings, double stops, and intricate combinations of slurs and single strokes. The first one to learn is usually the *shuffle bow*.

## Playing in the Higher Positions

Someone playing simple hymns for church, Christmas carols, fiddle tunes or folk music can usually play most everything in the first position, but to play more advanced solo pieces, chamber music and orchestra literature, one needs to be able to play in the upper positions.

## Sight-Reading

Good sight-reading skills are absolutely essential for playing in the pit orchestra of an opera, operetta or musical. Often there are only a few rehearsals and hours of music to be played. A good sight-reader who does not have a great tone will be more highly valued than a player with a gorgeous sound who can't read fast enough to play the notes.

## The Ability to Memorize Music

Being able to memorize music is a great help, but not essential for certain goals. If an orchestra player is a good sight-reader, they could still play well without memorizing anything, but if your goal is to be a strolling violinist in a restaurant, you need to learn how to memorize, and to cast romantic looks and flirtatious smiles while playing as well! (Conductors don't appreciate this skill in orchestral players.)

## Understanding Harmonic Structure and Tonalities

Understanding harmonic structure is important when doing improvisation. If you don't know the scale and basic arpeggios in the key you are playing in, you won't have much to contribute. Knowing the chord progressions will enable you to plan for what is coming up.

## Transposition

Being able to transpose is a skill rarely or never used by orchestral musicians, but is a great asset if you are playing folk music or popular music with singers. A guitarist can move her capo up or down a notch, but that might not be so simple for a violinist to adjust to if you do not have good solfege skills.

## Playing In Difficult, Uncommon Keys

If you want to play hymns in church, fiddle tunes or Bach minuets you will only need to be able to play in a few keys, but if you play in a **pit orchestra** for musicals or other shows with singers, expect to see key signatures with five and six sharps or flats. There won't be much time to think before the key changes, so you need to know your finger patterns and the positions that will suit those keys. If you intend to play for a summer theater, spend some time on the fingerings for the less common keys.

## Focusing Your Hearing

We all are aware that our eyes switch focus when looking from something close to something far away. We can also focus our hearing at different distances. This skill is especially important when playing a supporting line while someone else has a melody, but it is also important whenever we are playing with others.

*Some examples of the importance of Focusing Your Hearing when playing chamber music:*

1. **Intonation**. The upper voices need to **tune to the lowest voice.** In a string quartet this is usually the cello line. The reason is that this is the way our ears hear naturally. A house is built on the foundation, and the harmonies are built on the bass.

2. **Phrasing.** Players need to be aware of who has the prominent line and to play in a supportive way. Often this means phrasing your own part differently than if you were playing your own part as a solo line.

3. **Fluctuating Tempos**. Supporting voices need to be able to adjust their tempo to match the solo line, especially if there is a ritard or other tempo change.

4. **Coordinating Rhythms**. When one part has fast moving notes, like 16ths, the people playing quarter notes need to synchronize their note changes with the faster notes. Likewise, duplets should fit correctly into triplets. If one part has a trill with *Nachschlag*, the other parts need to hear that *Nachschlag* before playing their next note.
Note: *Nachschlag* is a German term, (literally "after hit"). An example is the two short notes—below and back to the main note—at the end of a trill.

**5. Hearing all the parts simultaneously** greatly increases our pleasure in fully appreciating the music. The composer was hearing all the parts. We play better when we hear the piece more the way the composer did.

Training your ability to

# FOCUS YOUR HEARING

away from the

sound of your own instrument

1. Using a metronome, play softly enough that you can hear every beat of the metronome quite distinctly.
2. Gradually play louder until you can play normally and still always hear the metronome.
3. Bit by bit move the metronome farther and farther away, always continuing to focus your hearing on it so that you can hear each click.
4. To make this more challenging, have someone keep changing the speed of the metronome. Be sure that you immediately change your speed to synchronize with the new metronome speed.

## *Auditioning well*

Presenting your abilities well in an audition is a skill in itself. If auditions will be required to achieve your goal (*examples*: getting into an orchestra or being selected for a scholarship) you will want to spend some time learning to audition well.

As a principal player in my orchestra, I was on the audition committee and learned a lot about who gets selected and why. I wished someone had clued me into to those things many years before!

See more about auditioning: page 191, Chapter 17, "Performing at Your Best."

## *Solo Playing*

For solo playing a beautiful tone, accurate intonation, and meaningful musical phrasing are the most essential skills.

The people listening to a soloist at church may not be very musically astute, but they will be very aware of a violinist's tone. If it is nasal, thin or scratchy they won't like it, even if the notes are played correctly. If the sound is warm, full and rich, they will. If, in addition, there is inspiration, emotional depth and exquisite musical phrasing, you might even get paid!

A soloist playing with an orchestra needs to have a tone that will be heard at the very back of the auditorium, even in soft passages. There may be twenty other violins playing at the same time, but the solo line needs to come through and be heard above all the rest.

## Having An "Outdoor Violin"

If you are going to play outdoor concerts, you will probably want to get a second instrument. This will be a big help when you face all kinds of weather conditions that would cause you great anxiety if you were playing your expensive, irreplaceable and treasured instrument.

## Have at least One Additional Bow and a 2$^{nd}$ Set of Strings

If you do any performing you need to have both a backup bow and additional strings. If a string breaks or the cork pops out of your bow you still need to be able to perform.

### *For Orchestral Playing: Rhythm is #1.*

If you play a note with a beautiful tone and accurate intonation, but you play it at the wrong time in the orchestra, your playing is not welcomed. Playing at the right time is the most important thing. Having your bowing match the rest of your section goes along with this.

If you are playing in a community orchestra and cannot play all the notes, you can still contribute by playing the notes that are possible for you. However, if you play at the wrong time or with poor rhythm, it will mess things up for everyone.

## Preparing your Orchestra Music
## More Efficiently

Get at least one recording of each piece of music. Having multiple recordings is better.

**Tapping along with the recording:**
Spend a large portion of your practice time tapping the rhythms of your part while listening to the recordings. Tap with your finger on the music and touch each note you will play with the same rhythm that you will play it. Sing along, if possible.

**This tapping trains:**
• your BODY memory of how to play it (tapping motion)
• your AUDITORY memory of how your part sounds
• your VISUAL skill at moving your eyes at the pace that is needed to keep up

If you cannot tap out your part with the recording, how can you expect your fingers and bow to play it?

Listening to the recordings also helps you to memorize the basic tempos for each movement and the tempo changes for different sections within them.

# Which Skill Sets Do You Need for Life?

## Lots of Options

We are blessed to live during a time where we have myriad possibilities and opportunities. Previous generations were limited to the people in their immediate surroundings, books, and letter writing. Then telephone, radio and movies were added, then television (with just a few channels), and now cable, satellite TV, the internet, mobile phones, text messaging, ebooks, videos, Skype, webinars... who knows what will be next?

The amount of information at our fingertips is staggering. People turn to YouTube for *How To's* and TED lectures for inspiration.

In the past, the way to receive an education was to attend a university or school. Higher tuition costs are now making that route less suitable for many, and online learning is beginning to make inroads into traditional education modes.

## Choosing how to spend your life-force energy and time

With all this available to us, it behooves us to make some conscious choices about what it is we want to learn, and which of these many information sources deserve our focus.

We are all given a limited number of days in this life, a limited number of hours and minutes. If we see it like a bank account that we are spending each day, each time we put our focus on something, we are using up some of our *life-account* on that. Are we spending wisely? Are we investing our life-force energy in a way that will bring us the skills and experiences which build in the directions of our desires?

## Career choices – what will be the linchpin?

What will be the linchpin that determines your choices in a career? Salary, location, work environment, environmental impact, work schedule, research opportunities, innovation, security, global benefit? People who discern what their priorities are, and live by them, can create much more satisfying lives.

## Story: A 40th Reunion

I watched a TV documentary that showed a group of men who met for their Harvard University 40th reunion. There were a number of interviews, and I was interested to see how differently the men had aged. One man, who particularly stood out, had gone to 3rd World countries to work as a doctor with people in profound need of medical care.

I was struck by the fact that his face looked so relaxed and peaceful, and he looked 20 years younger than his fellow classmates. My guess is that he had chosen a career path that was in line with his pure desires, instead of being swept into the rat race of trying to compete for things which would not bring him satisfaction.

## *Which skills do you need?*

In the same way that it is good to look at which skills we will need to achieve our goals on the violin, we can evaluate which skills fit into our overall goals in life.

If you are entrepreneurial, like the young man with the piano business in Chapter 1, spending your time and money on a college degree may not be the best use of the time in your *life-account* or the money in your bank account.

The innovators of today are working with technology that their professors cannot teach them about because it did not even exist 10 years ago. Where will you find the teachers and mentors who will best be able to guide you in your pursuits?

If you want to raise a family, what sorts of skills will be important for that and what sorts of career choices would suit that?

If you want to run your own business, what skills, contacts and credentials will you need?

If you want to work for a large company or the government because of the benefits, what will they be looking for when they choose employees?

If you want to be flexible with your location, you may want to consider accounting, an online business, or some other type of job which is not local dependent.

◆◆◆◆◆◆◆◆◆◆◆◆◆◆◆◆◆◆◆◆◆◆◆◆◆◆◆◆◆◆◆

# CHAPTER FOUR

# How does it go?

When musicians play a piece of music, they have a *sound idea* in their minds. One musician described it as a little man playing in his head and he is trying his best to play it just that way. Another described it as a recording playing in her head which she tries to match as she plays.

Both these musicians are quite clear about what they are striving for. Less advanced players often are not so sure. Instead, they may play the notes that are written as best they can, and then find out what it sounds like – thus formulating their idea of the piece that way.

Unfortunately, what can happen is that as they are learning the piece, they play out of tune or with the wrong rhythms (or both!). This becomes their personal version of the piece. If they then want to play it correctly, they have to *unlearn* their own personal version (which is harder than it was to learn it in the first place) and replace it with the correct rhythms and good intonation.

One of my teachers joked that no one can play Mozart in tune because when we first learned it we were students. Later, when we play it as mature musicians, we revert back to our previous mistakes and weaknesses in performing it.

> The clearer we are about
> what we want it to sound like,
> the easier it will be to play it that way.

## CREATING YOUR "SOUND IDEA"

### 1. Figure out the rhythms.

Before playing a new piece, take some time to figure out the beats and subdivisions for any complicated rhythms. This is especially true in slow movements that have 32nd and 64th notes interspersed with long notes.

### 2. Tap & sing the rhythms.

Be sure that you can tap and sing all the rhythms in your piece correctly while using a metronome. Pay extra attention to any complex rhythms that are not what you would expect them to be.

### 3. Subdivisions on long notes.

On long notes, make a mental imprint of what the subdivisions should be. For a whole note, say out loud (and later think) 4 sets of 16th notes. You may want to use a 4-syllable word, like "pepperoni."

### 4. Rests.

During the rests, count out loud. If possible, sing what someone else is playing during your rest while tapping the beats at the same time.

**5. Subdivide before playing 16ths.**

If you have a series of rests and will play 16th notes when you come in, in your mind begin counting the 16th note subdivisions in the preceding beats before you play. Also do this if you are playing long notes before the 16ths.

**6. Sing the intervals.**

Check that you can sing all the intervals that you will play. Put it into a range that suits your voice.

**7. Know the sound of the next note.**

You need to know what the next note will sound like while you are still playing the preceding note. You can train this by singing the next note out loud while still playing the previous note. It can be easier to do this with the piano, instead of singing while playing the violin.

**8. Musical phrasing.**

To improve your musical phrasing, sing each phrase in a faster tempo. Once you can sing it easily in a very fast tempo, the whole phrase will make more sense to you. You will get the big picture of how it is shaped, where it is going, and the overarching concept that is being expressed.

Next, slow it down incrementally so that you hear how the details begin to fit into the whole phrase as it gets slower.

It is something like watching a video of an athlete doing a particular move and then seeing it in *super slow motion*. Create phrases that have that same smooth and unwavering path to their destination.

## CREATING A "FEELING IMAGE"

**Imagine the muscle movements.**

In addition to hearing just what you want to play, there are tremendous advantages in imagining the muscle movements that you will do while playing.

It is said that the famous violinist, Niccolo Paganini, did much of his practicing lying on the couch.

### *Story: The Paganini Practicing Technique*

There is a story of a man who thought he could discover Paganini's magic by eavesdropping on his practicing as he prepared for a concert. The man was quite puzzled when he heard no sound at all. When Paganini was asked why he was not practicing, he replied that the way he practiced was to go over it all in his head.

If you can visualize exactly what and how you will play – the fingering, bowing and sound – your ability to play a piece will soar!

> The more advanced a musician becomes,
> the more music
> he can hold in his mind at once.

## A CONCEPT OF THE WHOLE PIECE

At first, we may only be able to know what the next few notes will be. Then we move on to holding a whole phrase in our minds, then larger and larger sections.

### Story:
### Hearing the Brahms Requiem in a New Way

When I was a music student in college, we performed the Brahms Requiem. I played in the orchestra for the performance, but also learned the alto part because one of the requirements for all music majors was to sing in the chorus. We worked on the Requiem for most of the semester, so with all those rehearsals I not only knew my own parts well, but everyone else's, too. By the end of the semester, I felt I knew that piece inside and out.

Later when I studied in Berlin, Germany, I went to a performance of the Brahms Requiem with Herbert von Karajan conducting the Berlin Philharmonic Orchestra. During that performance, I experienced the Requiem in a new way.

I hadn't realized it, but in my mind the individual movements were quite separate. For me it had been as though each movement was a piece unto itself and they were just played one after the other.

As Karajan conducted, I experienced the whole Requiem as one large piece. All the movements still had their own individual integrity and beauty, but now I heard how each belonged within the larger whole, each one adding to it and at the same time fitting within it.

It was magnificent.

I also knew that Karajan had been holding the entire Requiem in his mind as he made his first down beat. Every note had its place in his all-encompassing vision of what that performance was to be.

Thank you to a legendary musician for giving me that profound experience and teaching me something about our human potential.

◆◆◆◆◆◆◆◆◆◆◆◆◆◆◆◆◆◆◆◆◆◆◆◆◆◆◆◆◆◆◆◆◆

# Holding a Clear Vision of What You Intend to Create in Life

Whether we are building a bridge, remodeling a kitchen, doing a presentation for our company or creating a prototype for a new product, the clearer our vision is of the end product, the easier it will be to bring about our desired result.

Athletes are particularly aware of this and are often able to easily measure the results. If it gives them a faster clock time, higher batting average, or lower number of strokes in golf, they can easily measure the effectiveness of working with visualization.

They can use visualization for rehearsing their moves in their minds (the way Paganini did), for seeing their desired outcomes, and for holding a sustained laser-like focus. They can also use it to develop and employ powerful metaphors that expand them beyond their previous limitations, best scores or timings.

### *Story: Winning at the Hurdles*

I remember listening to an interview with an Olympic athlete who had won a hurdle event. He said that what was different about his technique was that his focus was on his time in the air instead of on the ground. In his mind, he was basically flying over the hurdles and touching down a bit in between each one. The strength of his flying image helped him to soar past the others and win each race.

## TECHNIQUES FOR EVERYDAY LIFE

People who are successful at creating what they want in life are usually very good at visualizing the outcomes they desire. Below are some strategies to help develop the skills of creating the life you want to be living.

The subconscious mind plays a major role in creating what happens in our lives. Therefore, to be most effective, the subconscious mind needs to be incorporated into any strategy for creating a desired outcome.

### Create impressions on the
### Subconscious Powerhouse of Creativity

Just before sleeping and immediately upon waking there is an overlap between full conscious awareness and the states of deep sleep and subconscious dreaming. This overlapping time is a window of opportunity to create impressions on the subconscious powerhouse of creativity. **The final thoughts before sleeping and the first thoughts upon waking are very potent.**

Here are some suggestions for utilizing those important times. The effects of doing these exercises are quite amazing and wonderful!

> A clear intent for the future
> combined with
> appreciation for what you already have
> is an unbeatable combination.

### In The Morning Upon Waking

**SHORT VERSION**

If you only have a short amount of time before starting your day, a **one-sentence general statement of intent** may work best for you. It helps to write it down and keep it in a handy place.

Declare your *general intent statement* three times either aloud or in your mind, then, as you begin going about your day think of at least a few things you appreciate about what is in your life.

**LONGER VERSION (*Morning*)**

If you have more time in the morning, you can declare your *general intent statement*, then run through a layout of your intentions for the day while interspersing it with appreciation for what you have – opportunities, material objects, physical capabilities, mental faculties, emotional pleasures, modern conveniences... There is a lot to appreciate and be grateful for.

## *At Night Before Sleeping*

Review your day, noticing what went well and what did not. If possible, use this as a time to ***investigate*** rather than to get emotionally worked up about things that bothered you.

### • Events that *Did* Go Well – What You Want *More* Of

Acknowledging and appreciating the events that you feel pleased about and are grateful for will help bring more of those situations into your life. Maybe a moment of beauty while driving to work was the nicest part of your day. Now that you realize that, you may find yourself paying more attention to the beauty around you, and thus having more of the experiences that please you.

### • Events that Did Not Go Well

When you find an event that was not what you would have wanted it to be, you can try the *TRANSFORMING EVENTS* exercise.

### • For the Future

Once the day has been reviewed – acknowledged, appreciated and cleaned up – you can also move into embedding desires for the future (mixed in with gratitude, for best results) into your mind before sleeping.

# TRANSFORMING EVENTS

## 1. Evaluate, find out
What about that event was not to your liking? Why do you feel bad about it?

## 2. What would have been better?
If you could do it over again, what would **you** do differently? How would you respond or act in a way that you now (lying in bed) would feel good as you think about it? If you had been feeling powerful, highly competent, skillful and/or loving, what would you have done in that situation?

If it is difficult to find how you wish you had acted, or what you think would be the best way to handle something, think of someone you admire and ask yourself what that person would have done. It could be someone you know, a public figure, a character you admire in a movie...

## 3. Rescript it & run the new version
Once you can think of a preferred scenario for the unpleasant event during your day, rescript it. Run the situation in your mind with the new preferred actions and outcomes. This will affect future events that have similarities to it.

## Negatives

The Statement of Intent should be in the positive. No use of words like *no, not* or *don't*. Unfortunately, the subconscious evidently does not understand negatives and just delivers whatever the literal meaning of a statement is without the negatives. "I *will not* screw up," becomes, "I *will* screw up."

## Story: "I won't screw up."

Someone sent me a card with a cartoon on the front. The picture is a percussionist standing in the orchestra wearing his concert clothes. Above him, the words in the thought-callout say, "I won't screw up. I won't screw up." In one hand is a cymbal and the other hand is held as though it is holding the other cymbal, but... it is empty. The caption below reads, "Roger screws up."

---

I think every musician has had an experience like this at some point. The more we say, "I won't screw up," the more likely we are to do just that.

◆◆◆◆◆◆◆◆◆◆◆◆◆◆◆◆◆◆◆◆◆◆◆◆◆◆◆◆◆◆◆◆◆◆◆◆◆

## The Best Strategy

Shortest Amount of Time

Least Amount of Effort

CHAPTER FIVE

# Meeting Challenges

Once we are clear how we want a piece to sound, and have practiced it for a while, it may start sounding pretty good.

However, what often happens is that parts of the piece are more difficult for us. Maybe the notes are too fast or awkward for the left hand, or maybe it calls for bowing techniques that we have not become skilled at yet.

Part of the fun of playing the violin is the satisfaction we get from meeting challenges and overcoming them. Knowing that we could not do something at first, but that now we can, is deliciously satisfying. "Hurray! I can do it!"

## STRATEGIES

Having a good strategy for meeting the challenges that come up can save us hours of hard work and frustration. It is like having the right tool when we are doing a home remodeling project. That electric sander, screw gun or power saw could make all the difference.

### The Most Common Strategy: "Try it again"

The most common strategy people use when something does not work, is to simply try it again. If it *does* work the second time, that strategy is fine. However, if it does not work the second time or 3rd time, one would do better to come up with a more effective strategy.

### Devising the Best Strategy

When a student comes into a lesson with a passage they cannot play, I like to first state our goal. What we are looking for is the strategy which will enable them to play that passage well – to be successful – in the **shortest amount of time with the least amount of effort.**

We then look to see what the problem is, and we devise a way to either fix it or to develop the skill they need to play it well.

### "What is it that makes it difficult?"

The best place to start is to analyze, "What is it that makes it difficult?" Knowing what is holding us back, will help us to devise a way to improve things. We want to address that particular weakness and not waste time and energy on other things.

A simple example of this from everyday life is a car that stops running. The mechanic looks for what the problem is, then fixes or replaces that part. If he was able to identify the cause correctly, the car will now work well again. No need to change every part in the car, just the one that was not working.

## Story: "I can't play it fast enough."

**Strategy**: Get the big picture, then fill in the details.

Bernie came into his lesson feeling frustrated about a particular passage in a piece he was playing with his chamber music group. It was a series of measures with running 16th notes. The tempo for the piece was set at what suited the group, and there wasn't any way they were going to play the whole piece at a speed which was comfortable for him to play that one 16th note passage.

He *had* to be able to play it faster. He had been working on it all week and had "hit a wall" with how fast he could play it. We needed a strategy that would take him beyond what he was able to do at home.

This is how we worked on it together.

Ruth: "OK, let's just get our baseline here so we can see how much you improve. Play it at **the tempo which *will* work** for you now, and we will see what speed that is on the metronome."

They find the speed that works and Bernie plays it at that speed correctly with the metronome. This is now his **departure point**. His **arrival point** will be playing it at the speed that the group is playing the rest of the piece (see Chapter 2: Setting Goals, page 13).

Ruth: "Now let's look at what makes this passage hard and what makes it easy."

In this case, most of the notes are stepwise (easy), the key is an easy one and it remains the same throughout (easy), it is all in 1st position (easy), the bow crossings are fairly minimal (moderately easy). So what is hard about it?

The real problem holding him back could be his ability to think the notes fast enough and know what was coming up. So it is not so much about getting his *fingers* to play fast enough. It is to train his mind to *think* fast enough.

Next is to come up with a strategy that will get Bernie to *THINK* the passage faster.

It would help if he knew what was coming up as he went along, if he knew all the notes. He could memorize the whole thing, but that would use up a lot of time and energy. **We want something faster and easier.**

Ruth: "Let's start by looking for any patterns that might show up."

This is an attempt to find a way to simplify it in his mind. In the same way that a series of words in a sentence are easier to remember than a series of random letters strung together without meaning, if Bernie hears the passage like words that make sense, he will be able to think through the passage faster.

It turns out that the passage is made up of four sections.
Each section is 16 notes long (four sets of four 16th notes).
Each section has a similar shape/pattern.
Note: There are four *sections*, 16 notes per *section* and 4 notes per *set*.

Ruth: "First, play the first note of each *section*."

Bernie does this a number of times. He is playing five notes – the first of each four sections and then the next down beat as an arrival point.

Ruth: "Play those five notes faster. Now memorize them."

Ruth: "Now play the whole passage as it is written, just to remember how it goes. Notice how you now know the first note of each section. *It is easier* because you know what is coming up."

Ruth: "Now let's look at each *section*. Is there a pattern that repeats from one section to the next?"

In this case the patterns repeat, and the first note of each *set* of four 16ths outlines a descending arpeggio.

Ruth: "Let's start with the first section. Play just the 1st note of each *set* of four 16ths. Notice the fingering. 1-3-1-3. Repeat that five times."

Ruth: "Now the 2nd section. Fingering is 0-2-0-2. Repeat that five times. Now the 3rd section (3-1-3-1), and the 4th..."

Bernie is playing the first note of each *set* of four 16ths, i.e., four notes for each *section*. Eventually he has memorized the fingering and can play all 4 patterns of arpeggios easily.

Because he is only playing one out of every four notes, it is easy for him to play much faster. The metronome is set much higher than when we started.

Ruth: "Now bow each of those arpeggio notes (the first of each set of 16ths) as a group of four 16ths on that *same note.*"

Bernie plays the passage a number of times with the faster metronome setting while playing 4 bows for each arpeggio note.

Ruth: "Now let's sing how it goes with the metronome."

This time we sing all the notes (as printed in the music) in the faster speed.

Ruth: "Now play it with the four bows on each note again, but in your mind sing all the notes (the way it is printed) as you play."

Ruth: "Now play it as printed."

*SUCCESS!* Bernie plays the whole passage correctly. He is very pleased when I show him that the metronome is now *five settings higher!* We look at the clock and note that the whole process took only **15 minutes.**

Follow up: Later, when Bernie played the piece during a chamber music coaching, he was able to play that passage fast enough. Hurray!

*A good strategy made all the difference.*
Bernie had tried all week to increase his speed with very little success. In 15 minutes he was able to increase it by five metronome notches. That was possible because **we solved the difficulty** of not being able to *think* the passage fast enough. It was well worth it to evaluate what was holding him back and address that specific issue.

*"Practicing is making SUCCESS a habit."*
Now that Bernie knows a strategy which enables him to play that passage fast enough, *his practice time should be used to solidify that success through repetition.*

**A Review of the Steps We Used:**

**1.** Establish where you are and what the goal is. Make it very clear what those both are by quantifying it.

*With Bernie, we marked down his present metronome speed and the goal metronome speed.*

**2.** Identify what the difficulty is.
If it is not working after the 1st try, why not? What makes it too difficult to do?

*Bernie: Couldn't <u>think</u> the notes that fast.*

**3.** Devise a way to isolate that problem, to address it specifically, and create a strategy that will enable you to supersede or override what is causing the difficulty (usually by simplifying it somehow).

*Bernie: Playing only the main notes and memorizing them would allow him to think through the passage much more quickly.*

**4.** Repetition, until that way of playing it is easy and smooth.

*Bernie: Played the main-note versions until they were easy.*

**5.** Imagine/visualize playing it with all the notes in the way you would like to.

*Bernie: Sang it in the goal tempo, then played the rhythms with the bow and imagined all the notes fitting in.*

**6.** Put the passage back into the context, play it as written in the goal tempo.

*Bernie: Played it as printed in the goal tempo.*

**7.** Celebrate when it works!

There are additional effective strategies in Chapter 6, page 59.

# Meeting Life's Challenges

Life is challenging at times, some times more than others, and for some people more than others, but we all face challenges. Because we each have our own unique personalities, how to best handle our challenges will vary. But one thing is for sure, **the better we are able to meet a challenge, the better we feel**.

Major challenges are beyond the scope of this book, but below you will find some ideas about challenges that you may encounter when attempting to attain a skill. For those, we can use similar strategies as we used for the violin.

## 1. Clarify your desired outcome

When things get difficult and our emotions start running on high, we can get so focused on the immediate challenge or difficulty that we lose clarity about what it is we *do* want.

Taking some time to write out or tell someone else what our desired outcome is can help a lot. Just thinking of it is also helpful, but our thoughts can be like *castles in the air* or lacking in substance. Expressing it in writing or to another person makes it part of the tangible world, which makes it more real.

*Example: I want to be fluent in French.*

## 2. Take an honest look at where you are now

The first step with Bernie (see page 45) was to find the metronome marking that he *could* play the passage. This was our starting point.

Taking some time to honestly assess your present situation is important. If we are not in truth about where we now are, it is hard to plot a good course to where we want to be.

*Example: I took French in high school, but I only got a reading-and-writing understanding of it. I never could speak it.*

## 3. Find the most direct path

Once we know where we are and where we want to be, we can often see the straight line that would be the shortest route between the two.

Question to ask: "How can I move there quickly and easily?" This helps us come up with a strategy.

*Example: I could go to France and participate in a total-immersion learning program.*

## 4. What will it take?

People often say, "Everything has its price." If we want to possess something which we presently do not have, there will be something required of us to have it.

To possess a skill, we need to practice it. If we want an item in a store we pay money for it. If we want our dog to be well behaved, he needs to be trained.

So once we see the most direct path to attaining our goal we also want to know, "What will it take to travel that path? **What will I need to do and invest?**"

If the investments are too high, we may need to change our path to accommodate that.

*Example: Since I cannot afford the time and money needed to do a total immersion program in France, I could buy a series of French language recordings, and listen to them each day during my 30-minute commute to work.*

### 5. Commit to the process, and test out that commitment

Knowing what actions we need to take, and that we are willing to do those, enables us to commit to the process.

That commitment solidifies when we start taking action to support it. *Doing a test is important.* If we find we can't seem to follow through, we are not really committed.

### *Story: Signing up for an Egypt tour*

When I started a business offering tours to Egypt, I learned very quickly that until people paid a deposit they were not really committed. An extreme example was a tour I hosted for two spiritual teachers. People signed a list saying they would be taking the tour. There were only 50 openings and 63 people signed up, but I thought it was likely some would not come through.

When I contacted them about sending in their $500 deposits, guess how many did? SEVEN. Lucky I had required a deposit before doing all the bookings!

In the same way that the tour deposit was only a portion of the total payment required, setting a *small goal* which takes us in the direction we want to go is a good test of our commitment. Do we follow through? Try the new exercise program for one month before buying the membership for a whole year. Take a few college courses before enrolling full time.

*Example: I buy one French language learning recording (not the whole set) and start listening to it each day. Do I follow through and keep it up consistently?*

### 6. Follow through, mentors & colleagues

If attaining the goal will take a longer period of time, a fair amount of fortitude will probably be required. This is where having other people to help us stay on track can be a big help.

Violin students can falter in their practicing if they do not have regular lessons. A personal trainer can benefit people in exercise programs. People in 12-step programs have a sponsor and group meetings to help them.

Being around other people who are actively working towards similar goals can be helpful. Exercise classes, team sports, mastermind groups, playing music in a chamber music group or orchestra – other people can help keep up our motivation and give us support and comradeship.

*Example: I join a French conversation group that meets twice a month.*

## Another Example of the Above Steps

From the story of Jacob learning the Bach Double Violin Concerto, pages 14-15:

### 1. Desired outcome.
Jacob wanted to learn the Bach Double.

### 2. Honest look at where he was.
He could not play it at all, so his starting point was zero.

### 3. Most direct route.
In Jacob's case it was to follow his teacher's instructions.

### 4. What would it take?
That he come to his violin lessons, pay close attention to what his teacher taught him and follow her instructions well. He would also need to practice for many, many hours at home.

### 5. Commit to the process.
In Jacob's case I told him we would try it for a few weeks and see if he had what it took to learn such a difficult piece.

### 6. Follow through, mentors and colleagues.
Jacob had regular violin lessons, so that helped him stay on track.

### What if I Don't See a Possible Way to Achieve My Goal?

Sometimes what looks like the best way to achieve our goals doesn't seem possible for reasons that we can't control. That can make us feel stuck.

### EXAMPLE: "I don't have the money..."

*I can't afford to go to France for an immersion program or even to buy a set of Learning French recordings.*

I could just end it there, with an "I can't," or I could think more creatively.

Possible solutions:
1. I might find some free French language learning sources on the internet.
2. I could get some recordings from the local public library.
3. I could find a native French speaker who lives locally and barter with her for French conversation lessons. Maybe she needs someone to clean her house or mow the lawn.

I might have to *think outside of the box*, more creatively than I did before.

### Is There An Obstacle?

If no creative solutions seem to be forthcoming, a question to ask is, "Is there some obstacle, something that is standing in the way?"

### *It's not me...*

Often the most spontaneous answer to that question is that some other person is the problem.

### *The place where you are the sovereign*

If at all possible, instead of saying that it is because of someone else, look for a way to change something *within yourself.* That is the place where you are the sovereign. **That is where we each have power.** When it comes to changing something within yourself, you are the one in charge.

### *"He won't let me."*

Many times people submit to someone else's whims without really testing it out. Sometimes letting someone else boss us around is a symptom that we just have not really gotten clear and focused within ourselves about what our intentions are. Instead, we let someone else make our choices. It can be a way of not taking the responsibility ourselves.

One way to take responsibility is to ask, "Is there something within *me* that is saying not to do it?" If there is, that will need to be dealt with. If there isn't, we can become clearer and firmer about what we intend to do.

Once we are clear and firm, other people will usually sense this and often either back down or just get out of our way. They may even come through with unexpected support, *especially if there is some benefit in that for them.*

### Story: He is happy to have me play the violin now

One adult violin student and her husband owned and operated a dairy farm. There was always more work to do and never enough hours in the day to finish it all.

At first, when my student began taking violin lessons, her husband didn't like having her take the time out to practice each day. However, when he discovered that playing the violin made her so much happier, and that when she was happy she gave him more of what *he* wanted (you can guess what), his attitude toward her violin playing changed.

◆◆◆◆◆◆◆◆◆◆◆◆◆◆◆◆◆◆◆◆◆◆◆◆◆◆◆◆◆◆◆◆◆◆◆◆◆

# CHAPTER SIX

# Effective Strategies – Where, Why, How?

This chapter includes a number of strategies for solving particular difficulties you may encounter in a piece you are playing.

**Challenge yourself with a fact-finding mission.**
Begin by playing it faster or slower, whichever is more difficult.

**1. Where does the problem occur?**
Isolate the problem spot.

**2. Why does it happen?**
Define the difficulty.

**3. How to fix it? Choose an "upgrade strategy."**
Devise a way that you *can* do it (see suggestions on the next pages).

## The UPGRADE PROCESS, Two Basic Approaches:
After defining what makes a passage difficult:

### 1. Change the Ratio Of Your Focus
Get the other aspects working first, so that you can then change the ratio of your focus while playing the difficult places.
or
### 2. Work directly on What is Problematic
Focus only on fixing the problem. Work on what makes it difficult, and make it easier by eliminating as many of the other aspects of executing it as possible.

### Approach #1:
### CHANGE THE RATIO OF YOUR FOCUS
### Solidify Everything Else First
Working on the aspects which are *not* difficult first, so you can later change the ratio of your focus.

When we play the violin, we are doing many different things at once. We are keeping track of:

- reading the notes (or is it memorized?)
- rhythms and counting
- bowing patterns
- bow distribution and where in the bow
- phrasing and dynamics
- articulation and tone
- finger patterns
- shifts and fingerings in the upper positions
- and more...

Evaluate, which of these are easy and could be put on autopilot?

By perfecting your ability to do the things which are *not* problematic, **you will then be able to put more focus on whatever the difficulty is.** That will make it more likely you can get the difficult places right.

*EXAMPLES of ways to make things more solid so you can change the ratio of your focus:*

**Memorizing**

If you have a passage memorized, you do not need to use any of your focus for concentrating on reading the notes. That means more of your attention can be directed towards monitoring your bowing or fingering, etc.

**Repetitive Bowing**

If the difficult passage uses a bowing pattern that repeats throughout the passage, you can learn that particular bowing on open strings or scales. This enables your bow arm to remember this as a known pattern. It becomes part of your *bowing vocabulary.* Now, when you play the difficult passage, you no longer have to use part of your attention for the bowing; the bowing is on automatic.

### Before & After the Difficult Place

Spend some time solidifying the notes both before and after any challenging spots. If you know the notes that precede a difficult place, you can use more of your attention to think ahead.

It is very common for people to stumble on the notes just after a difficult spot, so it is important to spend some time getting very solid on those notes, even if they seem easy.

## Approach #2:
## WORK DIRECTLY ON WHAT IS PROBLEMATIC
## by Making It Easier

Possible strategies for the following difficulties:

- INCREASING YOUR SPEED
- DIFFICULT STRING CROSSINGS
- DIFFICULT FINGERINGS
- LONG BOWS – SLURS or LONG NOTES
- SHIFTING

## INCREASING YOUR SPEED

### Possible strategies:

### 1. Gradually Increase the Speed
Play it at an easy tempo. Do at least three correct repetitions (in a row) in that tempo – it should feel easy – and then move the metronome up one notch and repeat the process.

### 2. Quantum Leap
Put the metronome on the goal speed. Play small sections at that speed. Choose the size of the section depending on what you *can* play at that speed. It may be just five notes!

Then string the sections into larger and larger sections. Include the first note in the following section so that you can chain link them together when you combine the sections.

### 3. Dotted Rhythms
(long-short-long-short & short-long-short-long)
This enables you to do a quick change between every other note. That is easier than playing every note rapidly.

Use the metronome and have it click in the space between each set of two notes. So with a dotted 8th plus 16th rhythm, the metronome is set on the 8th note. While the metronome clicks you should be thinking TWO notes at a time (the 16th and the following dotted 8th).

The short-long-short-long is more difficult, so spend extra time on that one.

### 4. Opposite Bowings

Make all the DOWN bows into UP bows. This will take some of your attention away from the left hand, which will make the **fingering more solid**. It will also mean your bow arm will be making the opposite ellipse for each string crossing, which will make the **string crossings** more obvious.

### 5. Think Faster

See the process for thinking the notes faster, as described in Chapter 5, pages 45-48, *I Can't Play It Fast Enough.*

### 6. Speed Up The Fingers

If you are having trouble moving the fingers fast enough, it can be helpful to spend some time on all the fingerings that involve *lifting* the fingers. The action of lifting a finger up is more difficult than putting a finger down.

### *Strategy:*

Use a metronome. There will be four clicks used for each note.
1.  For 3 clicks keep the finger *down*
2.  Then *lift it quickly on exactly the 4th click.*
Careful that the lifting motion is from the base of your finger, don't lift the finger only at the tip. The finger should remain in the same curled position when it lifts off.

Go through the whole passage that way (hold-hold-hold-change notes...). Make the finger changes lightning fast and exactly on the metronome click. Careful not to anticipate the click.

Also see the *Dounis* method for some good exercises to increase left hand facility.

---

### Exercises to Improve Left Hand Facility

D. C. Dounis devised a set of exercises, The Violin Player's Daily Dozen.

He isolated the three basic movements of the fingers:
- up-down (lifting/dropping down)
- sliding (up/down the string)
- sideways (from string to string – trained using left hand pizzicato)
- plus, holding a finger in one place

The Dounis exercises can seem like a wonder drug. However, they can be quite strenuous for the hand and tendons in the forearm, so should be used in small doses!

---

## SHIFTING

See Chapter 8, page 94-97, for a process to enable you to do big shifts confidently and effectively.

See also, "Learning to Shift," pages 122-124, 130, and 154.

# DIFFICULT STRING CROSSINGS

## *Possible strategies:*

### 1. Open Strings Only

Play the passage on open strings. Using the bowing as printed and the correct rhythms play each note on the proper string (without doing any of the fingering).

### 2. Sections Based On String

Divide it into sections based on which string the notes are on, not on phrasing. Add a rest between each string crossing.

### 3. Individual String Crossings

Play only the two notes that are part of the string crossing and play them over and over in the part of the bow it occurs in the piece. Notice which ellipse your arm and wrist make for the crossing. See if you can minimize the movement and make it more graceful and smooth.

The **String Crossing exercise** in the box on page 67 shows a good way to perfect these ellipses.

### 4. "Grab" Each New String

When you make a string crossing, "grab" the new string with the bow. Be sure that each time there is a new string you make a "K" sound with the bow. Use this both when the string crossing occurs in a slur and with separate bows.

### 5. "Backwards" Bowing

Reverse the bowing. Make all the DOWN bows into UP bows. This will challenge you to be more aware of the string crossings and will "wake up your bow arm" in a sense.

### 6. Change Your Bow Hold

• **Hold the bow in your fist** instead of with the fingers. This will tighten your wrist and force your arm to move more.

• **Move your bow hold up the stick closer to the balance point.** Having less weight will loosen your wrist and fingers on the bow and give you the experience of playing the string crossings more freely. Some fiddle players hold the bow this way, which enables them to easily do rapid bow crossings.

### 7. Tip-Middle-Frog

Challenge your bow arm by playing the passage all at the tip, the middle and then the frog. This will perfect the string crossings by making them more obvious and employing different parts of your bow arm – upper arm, forearm, wrist and fingers. That way all parts of your bow arm are working and ready to do their part.

### 8. The Choke – a remedy to produce resonant tone as well as correcting poor string crossings.

Loosen the bow a little bit and then play with full weight on the string for each note. Keep a steady heavy weight that produces a choked quality to the sound.

*Every* note should have the same sound. If any note sounds normal, that means you did not have your weight positioned clearly on the string. Those are the notes where you are unintentionally losing the full contact with the string when you play normally.

Note that you are *not pressing* with your bow-hand fingers. Your bow hand should remain supple. ***The weight comes from your arm.***

### Exercise to Improve
### String Crossing Ability

A good way to improve your ability to do any string crossing is to practice the eight combinations of four notes. Use the metronome and work it up to progressively faster speeds.

Keep track of your progress each day by recording the metronome speeds.

**Combinations**, using D and A strings as an example:
1) DAAA   2) DDAA   3) DDDA   4) DADA
5) ADDD   6) AADD   7) AAAD   8) ADAD

Start DOWN bow and emphasize the first note in each 4-note group. This is important to retain the meter (to make it clear which is the first note of each group).

## DIFFICULT FINGERINGS

See also the section, *IMPROVING INTONATION – It's All About Relationships*, Chapter 10, pages 119-124.

## INTONATION: Just ONE NOTE out of tune

If one particular note tends to be out of tune each time you play a passage.

*EXAMPLE: If you are playing a series of nine notes, and it is the 3rd note which tends to be out of tune.*

### Strategy:

**1. Find the correct location for note #3.**

Use a tuner so that you find it on the fingerboard and also hear it correctly.

**2. Be sure that note #2 is also correct.**

**3. Practice going from note #2 to #3.**

Keep going back and forth. *Memorize the relationship* of one note to the other. You need to know this relationship both if the 2 notes are on different strings or on the same string.

**4. Put it back in context.**

Play all nine notes. Did it work now?

People are less likely to be sure of the relationship between two notes that are on different strings. Because these multi-string relationships can be less obvious, they are even more important to practice.

# INTONATION: A SERIES of NOTES that are difficult to play in tune

## *Strategy:*

### 1. Familiarize yourself with the passage.

Play it through and look for the following:

- Look to see if the passage contains parts of any arpeggios or scales you already know.
- Notice your finger spacings and relationships.
- Look for notes that can be a "home base" (a note you are confident of and can use as a solid place from which to gauge the spacings to the other notes).
- Notice if there are notes which resonate with any open strings.

### 2. Simplify it, play it as all even notes

Simplify it so that your full concentration can be on getting the notes in tune. Do this by playing every note the same length. Every note is then a quarter note, regardless of its length in the piece.

Choose a metronome speed at which you can be successful. It is important to play rhythmically because when you play it in context you will want your fingers to move with precision at just the right time. You can make it easier by going slower, but you don't want the fingers to lose their rhythmic integrity.

### 3. With the rhythms as printed.

After you can play the passage successfully as *all quarter notes*, try playing it with the rhythms as printed. Still keep a slower tempo (with metronome) so that you have time to get it right.

### 4. Isolate difficult spots.

If there are now particular places that don't work, isolate those places, work them out, and then put them back into the context of the whole phrase.

## DOUBLE STOPS

The natural inclination when trying to play two strings at once is to press down more with the bow. This can result in some pretty ugly sounds and doesn't usually work out very well.

### Bow Level

What *will* help is to find the arm and elbow-height which allows you to move the bow at the level where you are resting on both strings equally.

Let your bow roll over the strings by raising and lowering your bow-arm elbow. Roll it slowly and notice how it feels when you are at that one level where you are touching both strings.

We do need to put down a bit more weight to get two strings resonating instead of just one, but it is not anywhere near as much as people are inclined to do if they do not have the bow in good contact with both strings.

### Bow-String Contact, Weight

Practice "grabbing" both strings with the bow, almost like doing pizzicato with the bow. This will make it clear if you are really contacting both strings at the same time. To be sure that your double stops will work in all areas of the bow, do this "bow plucking" near the frog, in the middle and at the tip.

## DOUBLE STOPS with ONE OPEN STRING

If you are playing double stops that involve fingered notes and an open string, you need to find a way to put your fingers down without touching the resonating open string. Double stops that include open strings are very common in fiddle music. An open string can also be used as a drone.

Possible options:

**1. Finger Placement.**
Instead of placing your fingers so that the strings are in the center of your fingertips, move them over, away from the open string, so that they are only partially on the string, but still enough to play the notes. You may even have to put your fingers on the fingerboard between two strings to get them out of the way.

**2. Finger Angle.**
Roll your fingers into a steeper angle so that they do not touch the neighboring string (which is the open string you are playing).

## DOUBLE STOP FINGERINGS

Learning it both vertically and horizontally.

*EXAMPLE:*
*Using letters to symbolize the UPPER notes – **A B C D**.*
*Using numbers to symbolize the LOWER notes – **1 2 3 4**.*

**Strategy:**
Repeat each of the following steps until it is easy. Then move on to the next step.

### 1. Play just the upper notes.
To familiarize yourself with the upper line.
*A B C D*

### 2. Play just the lower notes.
To familiarize yourself with the lower line.
*1 2 3 4*

### 3. Focus on each set of double stops.
Be sure that you are very clear on the relationship of the fingers. Find just the right relationship. **Play each set of double stops with multiple bows.** Play with a loud, clear tone so that you can hear the difference tones (the third note that we hear when two notes are played together in tune).

*A+1*, then *B+2*, then *C+3*, then *D+4.*

### 4. Introduce rhythm.
Use the metronome. Play each set (as above) for 2 bows, then 2 rests and then the next set. During the rests prepare the fingers for the next set.

Remember:
• the feeling of the relationship of your fingers
• the sound you want to hear
• imagine yourself playing it before you actually do.

*A+1*, rest-rest (prepare), *B+2*, rest-rest (prepare), *C+3*, rest-rest (prepare), *D+4.*

## 5. Play only the upper or lower line, but still do the double-stop fingering.

Play each note one time with one rest (with metronome).

*A(+1), rest (prepare), B(+2), rest (prepare), C(+3), rest (prepare), D(+4).*

Then:

*(A+)1, rest (prepare), (B+)2, rest (prepare), (C+)3, rest (prepare), (D+)4.*

This will give you a chance to hear the melodic lines and make some choices about which note to favor to gauge the intonation of each interval (double stop).

You will probably not want to play with equal temperament, but rather with the double stops in harmonically perfect intervals or *Just Tuning.** This will mean that you will have to move some notes up or down slightly. Decide now about which note will be the guide. The other note will then need to adjust to the guide.

*See *Just Intonation* at "Tuning Double Stops," page 120.

## 6. Repeat Step 4
## 7. Repeat Step 5

Keep alternating back and forth between Steps 4 & 5 until you feel you can play the passage with ease. If there are difficulties, you may need to work on just two pairs of notes at a time.

## 8. Play the passage without the rest in between the notes.

You will probably need to put a short space between each pair, then work at making it more legato.

*A+1, B+2, C+3, D+4.*

## LONG BOWS – SLURS or LONG NOTES

### *Equalize Bow Distribution & Sound Quality*

The natural tendency when playing a series of notes on one bow is to use more bow on the first notes, which makes us choke on the last notes. Perfecting the bow distribution and equalizing the quality of the sound on all the notes will improve this.

*EXAMPLE: Eight notes on one bow, with the natural tendency. The bow gets used as:*
*1st note : 30%*
*2nd note : 25%*
*3rd note : 20%*
*4th note : 10%*
*and the last 4 notes have only 15% left.*

When we think of it logically, it is obvious that each of the 8 notes should each have about 1/8 of the bow, but it doesn't end up happening that way unless we train it. No need to think of this as a personal problem, as it seems to be universal!

## EQUALIZING BOW DISTRIBUTION

### "Kay-Kay"

**1.** Get some artists' tape, used for watercolors, at a local art store. The one I have is white, about ¼" wide and in a roll. This tape is designed to be easily removable, something like the *Sticky Notes*. It works well for sticking on the wood of the bow and the fingerboard, and then being easily removed without harming the wood.

**2.** Use strips of the artists' tape to delineate the length of each stroke.

*Note:* **If you put the tape on the bow lengthwise**, instead of making little markers, it is more obvious, which makes it much easier when you are playing. To delineate 8 notes, make a checkerboard pattern going up the bow using four pieces of tape.

**3.** At the beginning of each 8 notes make a "K" sound with the bow.

So the 8 notes are: "**Kay-Kay-Kay-Kay-Kay-Kay-Kay-Kay.**"

## IMPROVING & EQUALIZING SOUND QUALITY
**Portato, "Wa-Wa"**

It is especially easy to lose sound quality on long bows. Use this exercise to improve the bowing on both slurs with many notes and long notes. It can also be used to improve your overall tone. The term for this type of bowing is *portato*.

**1.** Work out the bow distribution as described above.

**2.** After the ""Kay-Kay-Kay..." is working easily, replace it with "Wa-Wa-Wa..." Do one "Wa" for each beat, or each subdivision.

The "Wa" sound is made by doing a *kneading/massaging* motion with the index finger against the stick. This is accompanied by supportive motions with the other fingers, especially the 3rd finger on the frog.

The forearm of the bow arm needs to remain rotated inward to maintain a solid contact on the string.

The bow stick should flex in and out as you do this. Loosening the bow a bit helps to make this easier.

Whereas the "Kay" sound can be compared to a complete stop at a STOP sign, the "Wa" sound is like what is called a *rolling stop*. The bow slows down before each "Wa," but does not stop completely. Note that the slowing down in bow speed is to get the most benefit from this exercise. However, when using the *portato* bowing in a piece, you will probably want to keep the bow speed even.

Listening to recordings of David Oistrakh will help you to hear how the portato can be used effectively. Notice the rich tone and expressiveness.

### *Note: For this exercise the "Wa" sound is not produced by pulling the bow faster.*

Pulling the bow quickly is the natural tendency when trying to produce this sound, but that is not what will benefit you for this exercise. The "Wa" sound is produced by the change in weight on the bow with the *fingers* of the bow hand.

# Effective Strategies
# for
# Achieving Goals
# In Life

In the same way that having a good strategy can save a lot of time and effort when overcoming a difficulty on the violin, an effective strategy can bring us much better results with any project we are doing in life. This can make the difference between reaching our goal or not, and also how much energy, time and focus are needed to achieve it.

## *Go for the Real Goal*

It is important to be clear on what the real goal is. Many times people can get stalled or off track by seeking something else which they are hoping will bring them what it is they really want. They think they need to have X to get Z, so all the focus goes onto X.

The strategy should be focused on what you really want, not the vehicle you think might take you there.

## EXAMPLE: *Earning Money over the Summer*

Joanne wants to make some money over the summer. She doesn't have a car and figures she needs to get a car to get back and forth to a job. She puts a lot of energy into figuring out how to get the car.

Although this makes sense, she is now putting all her focus on *the car*, rather than her true goal which is to make some money. She may spend half the summer looking for a car, borrow money to buy it, work for another month and at the end of the summer just barely pay off the car before it breaks down.

*Result: At the end of the summer she ends up with no money (and no car).*

---

It would have been better to start by focusing on the true goal -- earning **money by the end of the summer**. There could be many options for achieving her goal.

### Possibilities:

• A job working from home – maybe online or by phone.

• Doing jobs for people in her neighborhood where she can bicycle or walk to them.

• A babysitting/mother's helper job where the parent brings the children to her or picks her up.

• A job where she does need transportation but can use public transport, company bus, bicycle... or she might have a relative that lives near the job and who would let her stay with them.

• A job that provides a company vehicle.

Whichever turns out to be the best way for Joanne, she wants to be sure that the result will be the money she set out to earn that summer.

## EXAMPLE: *A Loving Relationship*

Sally wants to have a loving relationship with a man. She's a bit overweight and thinks that for her to be attractive to a man she needs to lose weight and have surgery to change her figure.

She puts a lot of time, energy and money into getting herself all fixed up, slimmed down and enhanced. Soon she looks like the picture perfect trophy wife.

Sure enough, she attracts a man, but... he doesn't exchange love with her. He basically was looking for the kind of woman that is like an accessory – a glamorous dish to have on his arm – and who would satisfy his sex drive.

*Result: Sally achieved the goal of losing weight and attracting a man, but she failed at achieving her real goal which was to have a loving relationship.*

---

### A better possible strategy:

### 1. Awareness of the probabilities

Sally needs to know that there are PLENTY of men in the world who want a supportive woman who loves them, cares for them and appreciates what they do. Many of them even prefer a woman with some softness and natural curves.

## 2. Start doing it right now on a small scale

If she wants to have a Loving Relationship, she can focus on what that would be on a small scale in each and every interaction that she has with another human being. Every interaction can be *an opportunity to practice treating a person with the love she wants to be exchanging on a daily basis with her man.*

## 3. Making adjustments and developing skills

As she practices, she may find that there are things she needs to develop or change within herself.

### *Possibilities of Skills to Develop:*

• Her ability to let someone feel that she likes them

• Acting in a way that people know that she is an ally

• How to be appreciative when someone does something

• To be *Wow!*-ed by someone's skills

These are all things that most men like.

Once the signal gets sent out into the ethers that there is *an appreciative, supportive woman who wants to share love with a man,* (and who will not be undermining, criticizing, demanding or whiny), Sally will have her pick!

---

### The Best Strategy:

### Keep your FOCUS on the REAL GOAL

---

◆◆◆◆◆◆◆◆◆◆◆◆◆◆◆◆◆◆◆◆◆◆◆◆◆◆◆◆◆◆◆◆◆◆

# CHAPTER SEVEN

# What Are You Practicing?

Whenever we are playing the violin, everything we are doing is being "recorded" in our body memory as well as our mental & emotional memory.

That includes:

- **Fingering** – the feel of the fingers on the strings, which notes you are playing, and the sound of the intonation (pitch).
- **Bowing** – the tone, dynamics and articulation, as well as the slurs and bow distribution.
- **Rhythm** – the length of the notes in relationship to each other and the tempo (speed).
- **Musical Ideas** that are being expressed – the phrasing and meaning of what is being expressed by the music.
- **Ease or Difficulty** in playing the piece – whether you find it easy, comfortable, challenging, fearsome or stressful.
- **Pleasure or Displeasure** in playing the piece – whether we are pleased and excited to be playing the piece or unhappy to have to spend time on it.
- **Inspiration** – whether you are inspired by it or not, if you think it is beautiful or dull, exciting or boring.

### Imprinting the Memory

It is best to make clear choices about what we are imprinting our memories with.

**It is not wise to just plow through a piece
without being aware of
what habits we are ingraining into ourselves.**

For example, a common mistake made by less advanced players is to begin playing a piece with rhythms that vaguely resemble the piece they are attempting to play, but which are not accurate. As they repeatedly play the piece with these inaccurate rhythms *they are unwittingly teaching themselves to play the piece with the wrong rhythms.* Not a smart way to spend your practice time.

What is really unfortunate is that later, they then have to use a lot of energy and time to *correct* the habits they have developed. Unlearning and then relearning takes much more effort than learning it the right way in the first place.

Be sure that
the way you are practicing something
will not embed habits
you will have to correct and unlearn
in the future.

## SIMPLIFYING, Making It Easier

When we first start to work on a piece, it is very likely that we will not be able to play all of it at the level we would like. We will need to simplify it in different ways as we are learning it. It is good to choose ways that will not have to be unlearned later on.

### "Safe" Ways to Simplify It While Playing Through a WHOLE PIECE

#### Slow it down

The most common way to simplify it is to slow it down. This gives us more time to think about what we are doing, and gives us a better chance at being in control.

**Use a metronome to help you stay honest with the rhythms**. It is very important to keep everything in its proper relationship to the surrounding notes. Just speeding up on the easy places and slowing down when it gets more difficult is instilling a bad habit that will have to be corrected later.

#### Play with all separate bows

If we make *everything* a separate bow, we can then add in the correct bowings later.

#### Play high passages down an octave or more

Playing a difficult high passage down in the lower positions is a good way to:

- be clear about what the notes are
- be sure what the finger spacings and relationships are
- train the ear to hear all the intonation correctly

---

> ## Warning
>
> It is not good to leave out *some* of the bowings but not others. It will be difficult to fix later. If you make a change to something, make that change to ALL the notes, not only to some of them.

## Leave out the ornaments

Leaving out all the trills, turns, and other ornaments will make things easier. These can then be isolated later, and once they are learned can be added in.

## Omit difficult passages, just first notes and sing

If at first there are notes that are too difficult to play in your overall tempo, and you want to play through the piece, don't change the tempo to accommodate them. That will just make an imprint of an irregular tempo in your memory of the piece.

Instead, just **play the first note of each measure or each group of notes and sing the notes you can't play yet** in your mind (or out loud). This way you will be training your mental memory of the piece without practicing any bad habits.

Afterwards you can isolate that one place and perfect it before inserting it into the piece.

There are many more ways to simplify, and I hope you will add more to this list. Everyone has their own personality and learning style, so each one of us can find the ones that work best for us.

## Ways to Simplify DIFFICULT SECTIONS
See also the many strategies in Chapter Six, pages 59-76.

### Bowing
Make all the notes separate bows (don't just leave out some of the slurs).

### Left hand
Play all of the notes the same length so that you can focus on the intonation (don't just slow down on certain notes or the hard parts).

### Shifting
If you need to add extra time to get the right note after a shift, put in a definite rest, 1 or 2 beats with the metronome, (don't just hesitate for an indeterminate amount of time).

### Rhythm
Slowing it down is often the best idea, but keep all the notes in the correct proportions to each other. No playing the long notes shorter just because you don't want to wait that long!

### Dynamics
If it is *forte* or *piano* you can practice it at a good healthy midrange dynamic while you are learning the notes and rhythms, but try to keep that consistent throughout.

Also, be careful not to take your weight off the string when the notes get more difficult.

## STOPPING ALONG THE WAY TO FIX MISTAKES

This is the "I'll just stop and fix that" or "I didn't get that right, I'll do it again." It is natural to do this, but it can become a disability. The disability is that the *person cannot play through the piece without stopping.*

It is an easy habit to get into. We hesitate, stop or repeat something that didn't work, even though we had planned to do a run-through as though it was a performance. We change our minds (after all, it's not *really* a performance...).

This is a tough one to fix once it has become entrenched. Here are two strategies to work on this problem.

### *Strategy #1: Don't Stop Exactly Where It Happens.*
### *FINISH THE PHRASE, and then Go Back and Fix It.*

The reason we do it, is that we want to make sure we have everything working well. Just plowing through and making loads of mistakes leads to pretty slopping playing, so we DO want to correct things as they come up. The difficulty comes because a person can lose the ability to keep going – even in a performance.

We can avoid this problem by simply always continuing and finishing the phrase or section we are playing. Regardless of the mistakes – *keep going until the end of the phrase* – then stop, go back and work out whatever is needed.

That way we still correct errors and reinforce our ability to play it right, and at the same time we strengthen our ability to push on through when there are difficulties.

During the bulk of their practice time, most people are working on improving or perfecting different spots. Strategy #1 would be used during that time. That is different than playing it as though it was a performance.

In a performance we need to keep going, even if we are not happy with how we just did something. If you are having trouble doing that, here is a suggestion.

### Strategy #2: Getting Through a Whole Piece Without Stopping or Repeating

1. Put the metronome on an easy tempo.

2. Resolve that you will keep going *no matter what.*

3. Turn on your recording device. This is a way not to fool yourself by forgetting that you repeated something or hesitated.

It becomes so second nature that people actually *forget* they have stopped or repeated. The power of our minds to overlook what we do not want to remember is strong.

4. Play all the way through, keeping pace with the metronome. Using the metronome keeps you honest.

5. Listen to the recording and make notes on the music where the problems occurred.

## Story: Breaking a Habit

A 10-year old student had fallen into the habit of stopping each time she missed a note or rhythm and doing it again to get it right before she continued. This was probably her basic mode of practicing at home.

In the lesson I asked her to play it as though it was the recital now (no stopping). She started out with great resolve, but soon she was stopping and fixing without even thinking. When she reached the end of the piece I asked her how many times she thought she had stopped and started something again.

She hesitated, "One, or maybe two?"
"Five."
"Really?"
"Yes."

We needed to find a way to fix this. She was a very bright kid, was responsible, and had a great attitude. She was sure she could fix this. She said she would show me she could do it next week, so I didn't push it.

Next week the same problem. This time it was agreed that when she practiced at home, she would use the metronome to help her keep going. She PROMISED she would get it for the following week. But the next week it was still the same.

We needed to employ a different strategy. I decided to try the **Reward/Loss** system.

I put 6 quarters on the music stand. "These are all yours now, but each time you stop you will lose one of them."

The effect was magical. I only needed to reach over and take a quarter off once. The second time she began to stumble I started to reach out my hand to take another one. When she saw the hand coming, she pushed her way through without stopping.

When she finished we celebrated and laughed about when I reached out to take the 2nd quarter and she became even more determined.

I really meant it when I said she could have the quarters that were left, but she refused to take them. I don't think the money itself was what made the difference. The money was just an obvious symbol of what was happening, and using it made it a clear challenge.

We talked about what would be the best way for her to be able to have the same success repeatedly at home. She volunteered that they could use her allowance as the money she would lose. I was surprised, but she wanted to do it that way. She really did have a strong desire to play it well.

When the recital came she was able to play through her piece without hesitations, and she did a great job. Hurray!

◆◆◆◆◆◆◆◆◆◆◆◆◆◆◆◆◆◆◆◆◆◆◆◆◆◆◆◆◆◆◆◆◆◆

# Forming Habits
# in Daily Life

When we practice the violin, we are developing abilities that we did not have before
and then solidifying them by repeating them. This repetition moves them into *habit status*. The sign in my studio says, "Practicing is making *SUCCESS* a habit."

When something becomes a habit, we do it without needing to think about it, and that can be very useful. It makes our lives smoother and easier because we need less energy and focus to get things done. It can also make our lives more difficult, if the habits are not good ones.

## FORMING GOOD HABITS

If we want something to be an easy, smooth habit, we need two things:

• consistency
• repetition

The more consistent we are and the more times we do it, the more ingrained and reliable the habit becomes.

*EXAMPLE: If practicing at the same time each day becomes a habit, it will happen much more easily and consistently than if you need to decide each day when you will practice.*

### Good habits can help us to avoid pitfalls.

When I locked my keys in the car more than once, my father pointed out that if I made it a habit to *always* lock the driver side door with my key, it would be impossible to lock the keys in the car. This was so obvious, one would think that I would have already thought of it, but I had not.

Now that I have instilled that habit, I don't use any time or energy to think about whether to use the key or press the lock, I just let the habit make that decision – and the decision is to *always use the key*. An easy way to solve that problem!

### Bad Habits

Breaking a bad habit that is already instilled is *a lot* harder than forming a new habit. Of course what is ideal is if the bad habits never get formed in the first place.

The more conscious we can be when we begin doing something new, the better off we are.

> ### Question
> When deciding whether to do something or not:
> "Would I want to find myself doing this unintentionally?"

◆◆◆◆◆◆◆◆◆◆◆◆◆◆◆◆◆◆◆◆◆◆◆◆◆◆◆◆◆◆

# CHAPTER EIGHT

# Embody the Feeling

Practice playing each passage with the feeling you want to have when you play it well:

## Confidence, Solidity and Ease

## LESS EFFORT ⇒ SPEED

**The less effort needed, the faster you can play.**
**Fast passages need to be played with minimal effort.**

When a car is traveling in first gear, it has more power to climb hills or get the car moving from a standstill. Using all that power, however, also means that the car cannot travel very fast in first gear.

If the car is in fourth or fifth gear it does not have as much power, but it can propel the car at much faster speeds.

Likewise, when we want to play a long string of fast notes, we need to be able to execute those notes with a minimum amount of effort (power). The less effort we need to play the notes, the faster we will be able to play them.

---

### Hint

Never let yourself get tight or tense when practicing a fast passage. Use the strategies in Chapters 5 and 6 to easily and gracefully work it up to a faster speed.

---

So when you are practicing a passage with the goal of being able to play it fast, the best way to practice it is in a slow tempo *while using the least amount of effort.*

As you need less and less effort to play it, you will be able to easily increase it to a faster tempo.

## BIG SHIFTS

### *Taking You Where You Want To Go*

The following is a process for helping you shift confidently to a note in a different position, either up or down. However, the concepts described here can be applied to any note which is an arrival point.

This can also be used to **solidify a cadence or climax note.**

There is more about SHIFTING in Chapter 10, *Upgrading your Overall Technique*, pages 122-124, "Learning to Shift," also pages 85, 130, and 154.

### *Strategy:*

#### 1. Pitch. Play the arrival note only.

Be sure that you can play the note you want to arrive on exactly in tune (use a tuner, if necessary) and with a good full rich tone.

#### 2. Dynamic & bowing style.

- Play the arrival note with the **same dynamic** (loud-soft) that you will play this note in the context of the piece.
- Use the **same articulation and bowing style** that you will want it to have in the context of the piece.

Notes played in the upper positions result in a shorter string length. This means you will need to play closer to the bridge to find the *Sounding Point* where the note resonates most freely. Playing closer to the bridge will mean more weight is needed on the string to produce a good tone.

Keep in mind the bow speed you will be using for this note. This will also affect the amount of weight, and hence how close to the bridge you need to play.

### 3. Rhythm, arrival note + following notes.

Beginning on the arrival note, play the arrival note and the following group of notes with the correct rhythm and in the tempo that it will occur in the piece.

### 4. Solidify this with repetition and satisfaction.

Starting on the arrival note, play the passage imbuing it with a feeling of satisfaction and sureness. Think, "Yes! Good," as you hit it just right.

*Note:* This is like the target shooter hitting the bullseye in Chapter 1. His pattern was: *Success, Rejoice, Satisfaction.*

### 5. Play (only) the notes that are before the arrival note.

Make sure they are solid. Stop just before the arrival note.

### 6. Add two beats of rest before playing the arrival note.

Using the metronome, begin at a convenient place before the arrival note and play the passage until you get to the arrival note.

Stop before playing the arrival note and add two or more beats of rest before playing it. Use these two beats to move to the note and prepare yourself so that you can play it with ease and confidence *just the way you practiced it in Steps 1-4*.

If this feels hurried, choose however many beats you need to feel comfortable and get it right.

**Hint:** During the rests envision playing the arrival note *before* moving to it and playing it.

- Hear it in your head.
- Know how it will feel in your fingers and bow.
- Remember the good feeling of playing it.

Once you have the whole thing in your mind, move to it and play. **"Yes! Good."**

### 7. Make it only one beat of rest.

Once you are solid and comfortable with the two beats of rest, make it only one beat of rest before the arrival note.

### 8. Sing the passage with the metronome.

To be sure that you can imagine how it will sound when you leave out the added rest. Singing it will help with giving you a clear *Sound Idea*. See page 32-36.

### 9. Sing the preceding notes, then play on the arrival note.

Only begin to play on the arrival note, sing the preceding notes. Play it with the same confidence and good sound that you perfected in Steps 1-4.

### 10. Play it as written.

Be sure that before you play the arrival note that you know just what you are about to do. Hear in your mind and envision your satisfying *Sound Idea*.

**When you feel that sweet success, ENJOY IT!**

## INSPIRED PLAYING

One of my friends is fond of saying, "The voice does not lie." What she means by that is that the *quality* of a person's voice gives away what it is they are truly feeling, the state they are really in. A person may say that everything is just fine, but the heavy sorrow in her voice will give her away.

Likewise, when we are playing music we are *expressing*. Your instrument is your voice. If you feel that the piece you are playing is boring, it will sound that way. If you are actually angry about something or feeling competitive, your playing will sound that way, too.

So to play in an inspired way, we need to *embody* the state of being inspired. If the piece calls for playing a passage with warmth or tenderness, we won't be able to convey that if we are focusing on how angry we are about something.

How can we embody the states we want to convey with the music? A person's *inner communication vocabulary* is unique to each one of us.

However, here are some ideas.

### • Putting Words to It
Make the melody into a song that is giving people a message or telling them a story.

### • Story Line
Let each phrase tell more about a story as it unfolds throughout the piece.

### • Characterizations

Choose a character from a book, movie or story, or make up one of your own. Imagine that character as you play. Hear them singing what you are playing or how their voice might sound.

*Examples: People, animals, cartoons, puppets.*

### • Visual Images

Picture scenes or visual impressions that bring up certain feelings or emotions for you.

*Example: A ray of sunlight coming through the clouds in a sky that is still partially dark from a storm.*

### • Body Feelings

Rocking, swaying, reaching, throwing, dancing, crouching, pushing, stroking something soft, breezes, cold, hot...

*Example: Swaying on a porch swing on a warm summer night with a light breeze and the smell of jasmine in the air.*

### • Memories

Go into your past memories and see if the character of the music reminds you of something from your life experiences.

### • Sound only, without tangible associations

Be in the flow of the pure sound as an experience that goes beyond physical life experiences.

### • Sound as a vehicle that carries you

In the same way that an airplane takes you to a new place or a river carries you to a different destination, sound can carry us to other realms and experiences. Ride the sound.

◆◆◆◆◆◆◆◆◆◆◆◆◆◆◆◆◆◆◆◆◆◆◆◆◆◆◆◆◆◆◆◆◆◆◆◆

# Embodying the Feeling

## The Most Important Component
## in Manifesting
## What You Want in Life

The most important key to Manifestation is to embody the feeling of having the experience that we want to achieve.

Some people describe this as, "If you believe it, you can achieve it." What they are saying is that when we are embodying the state of what it is to have something (they call this "believing" it) that opens the door to having it happen. It puts us on that wavelength, or tunes our radio to that station.

I always found it impossible to believe that something was true before I knew it actually was. I associated that sort of "believing" with people being gullible, lost in fantasy, and full of wishful thinking.

Now I see that it was their way of describing the concept, "We need to embody the state of having-that-which-we-want-to-achieve."

### More Money

If we want more money, the solution is to start embodying the *feeling of abundance.* We can do that by constantly noticing all that we *do* have and feeling the satisfaction that we have so very much. Religions try to guide us in this by teaching us to give thanks and be grateful.

A simple way to increase your money supply is to start and end each day by listing ten different things you have that you are grateful for. If you use each finger individually, it helps keep track of how far you have gotten in the process. As you think of each thing, let the feeling of gratitude and pleasure in *having it* fill you. You are practicing being rich!

### Better Relationships

If you want better relationships in your life, you can follow a similar process. For each of your ten fingers remember a time that you felt really good about someone and enjoyed being with them. Recall as much detail as you need to feel that wonderful feeling again.

### More Love

Of course it is easier to feel love for other people when they love us, but their love for us is actually happening inside *them.* It is their experience, not ours. The experience we are really seeking is to *feel the love ourselves,* and we just want other people to make it easier for us!

If you want to have more love in your life, you can follow the same process. As you go through each finger, focus on a different person and let your love flow to that person. You can also focus on animals, places or anything else that you feel a loving connection with.

You can focus on past experiences of how you felt when you were spontaneously aware of how much you loved someone. Notice how it felt in your body and any words that came to mind.

You can use the feelings from the present, past or future. The important thing is to embody the feeling of *having the love within you* as you focus on it now.

You can practice feeling love any time you would like, and you can feel love for anyone or anything. No one can stop you from that. When it only exists within *you*, that is your sovereign realm.

> **When we practice**
> **Embodying Something Repeatedly**
> **we get better at**
> **Doing It and Having It.**

◆◆◆◆◆◆◆◆◆◆◆◆◆◆◆◆◆◆◆◆◆◆◆◆◆◆◆◆◆◆◆◆◆◆

# CHAPTER NINE

# Repetitions and Erasing Mistakes

Mistakes are part of the package called *Trial and Error*. It is the most common way to learn a skill. If we don't try, we never even get to enter the game. And if we do try, we will make mistakes.

Most of this book is filled with ways that we can work from success to success. That is certainly the best case scenario and one well worth striving for, but mistakes do happen. This chapter gives some ideas on how to best deal with them.

## BASIC CONCEPTS

### 1. Accept it and see it as valuable information

It needs to be accepted that something *was* a mistake, and without a defensive attitude or chip on the shoulder. It is valuable information, not an affront to anyone's value as a human being. . .

*Example: I just played a note that didn't sound right (that does not mean, "I am a horribly flawed person").*

## 2. How can that information be used to my benefit?

The best response to the mistake is to see what information it has for us. One thing it usually does is to clarify what it is that we *do* want. If that note was not right, what *is* the right note there?

*Example: I just played an F#. Oh! It was supposed to be an F natural.*

## 3. What allowed that to happen?

X did not work. Why not? Where and what is the weakness that allowed that to occur?

*Example: How did that happen? Oh, I see. There was an F# in the previous measure, so I continued to play the next F as a sharp, too.*

## 4. How can this be avoided?

What needs to change for this not to happen in the future? What is the correct way and how can I develop the ability to do that?

*Example: I'll write a natural sign above it to remind myself.*

## 5. What do I need to do to erase the mistake?

*Example: I will play that measure 5-10 times in a row correctly, just to be sure of it.*

## 6. Making it work right every time in the future

How do I develop the skill to do this well each time I encounter it in the future?

*Example: After playing that measure 5-10 times correctly, I will go back and start at the beginning of the phrase. I will also look to see if this occurs anywhere else in the piece (and practice those as well), so I can be sure to get it right each time.*

## "ERASING" TECHNIQUES

The basic idea is to log in many more **correct repetitions** to cancel out the mistakes. A lot of correct repetitions will be needed. If I make a mistake twice, I may need to play it 20 times correctly to fully erase it.

**Note:** You don't want the last time you play it to be one of the failures. It is always better to end with success.

### STRATEGIES to Solidify Accuracy
### (Erasing Mistakes)

### Logging In 100 Repetitions
By the time you have played something correctly 100 times, you know it. It is like a pilot who logs in flight time, or a driving student who is required to drive a certain number of hours before getting a driver's license.

See also the **1,000 Repetitions** from the Suzuki Violin Method, page 143.

### Game: Each Mistake = 2 More Repetitions Needed
*Example: Goal is 10 correct repetitions.*
The first 3 go well. Score is now 3. We need 7 more.
4th try is wrong. Ooops! Now we need 9 more. . .

### Game: Get Them All or Start Over
• You have to play it correctly 5 times in a row.
• If you mess up on #4, you have to start from #1 again.

*Note:* The kids seem to really enjoy the two games above, probably because it is so obvious and concrete. When they achieve it they can *know* that it has been achieved (and, of course, there is a lot of celebration when they do). It is nice when something is measurable, and it is a great feeling to be able to check off that box and know they got the goal. Hurray!

### Testing if the mistake has been erased

Be sure you can play it many times *in a row* correctly. If it is three times right, one time wrong, two times right, etc., it has not been erased yet.

◆◆◆◆◆◆◆◆◆◆◆◆◆◆◆◆◆◆◆◆◆◆◆◆◆◆◆◆◆◆◆

# Mistakes, Apologies & Forgiveness in Life

### *"Erasing" Mistakes, Atonement*

Erasing a mistake in life is not as simple as on the violin. Different religions have ways to help people with this. Doing penance, enduring a punishment, atonement... none of that is for this book to address. Instead, here are some ideas about apologies and forgiveness.

## Apologies

It is hard to imagine a relationship where an apology will not be called for as some point. It can be hard to do, but it is well worth it.

## Forgiveness

For most people forgiveness comes spontaneously when they realize that the other people have reached a point where, if they were presented with the same situation again, they would handle it differently. This can also apply to forgiving ourselves.

## Changing for the better is what really matters

I think one of the main misconceptions that we are given about apologies is the idea that the important thing is to be *really* sorry, to feel just awful and angry at ourselves.

If we step out of the emotional aspect and just look at that logically, how does feeling bad really solve anything? Only if it brings us to a place of making some sort of change.

### Example:

If Harold feels terrible about what he does to people when he is drunk, does his feeling bad make it any better for the people who suffer because of his behavior? The worse he feels, the more he drinks, and the more damage is done.

On the other hand, if he changed his behavior, albeit because of his regrets, it would be a lot better for everyone.

> **Regret can be the impetus for change,
> but it is not an end in itself.**

## *What's a Good Apology?*

If someone "does me wrong," hearing a lot about how bad it makes *them* feel actually makes it more about *them*. What they did probably had selfish motives in the first place, and making the apology about how *they* feel just continues that.

We probably do want to see that they regret it, but we also need to hear and see that **they are going to change** and to **make up for what they have done.**

Below is from an email that went around. It certainly spells it out.

---

### An Apology Includes Explaining . . .

- What you did that was wrong and why it was wrong

- How you will change your behavior to prevent it happening again in the future

- How you will remedy or compensate for the harm you caused by your action

### And the Understanding . . .

- That forgiveness is not an entitlement

- That there are always consequences for our actions

~ Postcards from the Edge of Insanity

---

CHAPTER TEN

# Upgrading Your Overall Technique

Whereas Chapter 7, **Strategies**, focused on solving specific difficulties that might be encountered in a piece of music, the topics in this chapter are skills that we work on over time to upgrade our violin playing abilities in general.

## *BOWING SKILLS in this chapter*
- KEEPING WHOLE-BOWS STRAIGHT.  Frog-to-Tip
  "Connect the Dots" For STRAIGHT BOWS
- VARIATION: *Kay-Sound "Plucking" Only*
- BOWING 3-NOTE CHORDS, Triple-Stops
- SPICCATO and BOUNCING BOWS

## *FINGERING SKILLS in this chapter*
- IMPROVING INTONATION
- FINGER SPACINGS / RELATIONSHIPS
- SCALES, ARPEGGIOS & THIRDS
- LEARNING TO SHIFT

## A SHORT "FORGETTING TIME"

### *How the Body Will Learn Most Easily and Quickly*

Unlike the mind, where we can cram a bunch of information in before an exam, the most important factor in training our bodies to perform a new skill is the *Forgetting Time*.

The *Forgetting Time* is the amount of time between when you did a particular action and when you do that same action again. If I practice a scale at 8am on Sunday and play it again at 10am on Monday, my forgetting time is 26 hours.

## The shorter the forgetting time the faster the body will learn.

For example, if you want to train your left hand fingering quickly, easily and reliably, the difference between playing it at 8am and 8pm the same day is 12 hours. But if you wait two days, it could be 48 hours or more. The difference is not that you will learn four times faster, it is much more than that.

**Note that you do not need to spend a lot of time on it.** The important thing is to have the shortest amount of *forgetting time* between your practice sessions.

This concept will apply to any skill you are teaching your body. It also applies to audio memory, such as learning a new language, or remembering someone's name when you first meet them.

## KEEPING WHOLE-BOWS STRAIGHT, Frog-to-Tip

The path of a straight DOWN bow (parallel to the bridge) is not a natural pathway that gets established doing anything else we do in life. Therefore, it is a new pathway for our arms to learn, no matter what age you are beginning to play the violin.

Here is one exercise that can help with executing a stroke that remains straight from frog to tip and back again. The idea is to *build from SUCCESS to SUCCESS*, perfecting each step and then moving to the next.

### *Exercises:*

### *"Connect the Dots" for STRAIGHT BOWS*
Establish what it is to play at the frog and also at the tip, then connect the two.

#### 1. Frog
Play sets of four 16ths at the frog. Keep playing them until you feel comfortable playing rapid notes in that part of the bow. Note that you will need to dangle your wrist a bit and play on the side of the hair. The wrist should be flexible.

#### 2. Tip
Do the same thing at the tip. Extra weight will be needed at the tip, and the bow hair will be flat to get a good, solid sound.

### 3. With Rhythm

Introduce rhythm (use the metronome).

• Beginning with a DOWN bow, play 4 sets of 16ths at the frog

• 2 beats rest during which you *lift the bow* and place it at the tip

• Play 4 sets of 16ths at the tip beginning with an UP bow

• 2 beats rest during which you lift and go back to the frog

• Repeat

### 4. Visualize the opposite end of the bow, then play whole bows in between the 16ths

Still using the metronome...

• Play two sets of 16ths at the frog beginning with a DOWN bow. As you are playing the 16ths at the frog, bring to your mind how it will feel to be playing at the tip. That is your destination. Think what it will feel like to be there at the tip.

• Then pull the bow *rapidly* to the tip (a whole bow stroke). Simply move to the tip quickly, easily and gracefully. The whole-bow frog $\Rightarrow$ tip will be on a DOWN bow.

• Then play 2 sets of 16ths at the tip starting on an UP bow. As you are playing the 16ths at the tip, bring to your mind how it will feel to be playing at the frog. That is your destination. Think what it will feel like to be there at the frog.

• Do a rapid UP bow (whole bow stroke) to take you to the frog. You are already imagining that you are there, and now just easily let your hand connect with your inner vision.

• Repeat. **Do not focus on the space in between the frog and tip, just on the two destinations (frog and tip).**

You are simply "connecting the dots."

### 5. Only one set of 16ths

Do the same thing but with 1 set of 16ths at both the frog and tip.

### 6. On the notes of a scale

Use this pattern on each note of a scale.

### 7. Whole bows only, with a "Kay" sound

Play the scale with only the whole bows (no 16ths), but add a "**Kay**" sound at the beginning of each stroke and a one-beat rest between the bow strokes (while you visualize).

• With the bow resting on the string at the frog, visualize what it will be like to be at the tip.

• Make a "**Kay**" sound at the beginning of the DOWN bow, moving quickly and easily to the opposite end of the bow (tip).

• Before playing the UP bow, put in a one-beat rest while you imagine being at the opposite end of the bow (frog).

• Make a "**Kay**" sound at the beginning of the UP bow, moving quickly and easily to the opposite end of the bow (frog).

• Before playing the DOWN bow, put in a one-beat rest while you imagine being at the opposite end of the bow, and so on.

## VARIATION of "Connect the Dots": Kay-Sound "Plucking" Only

**Steps 1-3 are the same.**

### 4. Replace the 16th notes with a *Kay-sound "PLUCK"*

• With the bow resting on the string at the frog, visualize what it will be like to be at the tip.

• Do a *Kay-sound pluck* with your bow, frog $\Rightarrow$ tip
"Grab" the string with your bow, give a tug which results in a "Kay" sound, and then lift it so it does not touch the string while you move rapidly frog $\Rightarrow$ tip.

• Do a *Kay-sound pluck* with your bow, tip $\Rightarrow$ frog.

• Choose a speed that works for you on the metronome, and proceed to **Step 7** as above.

**Connect the dots!**


The beauty of this exercise (and the variation) is that it circumvents the clumsiness that comes when we try to monitor traveling in a straight line with the bow. Think of the graceful, direct way that a karate master will move his hand and arm. There is no fumbling along the way.

What a good feeling when you can move your bow with that same assurance and expertise!

## BOWING 3-NOTE CHORDS, Triple-Stops

The interesting thing about producing warm, vibrant 3-note chords is that we have to work against our natural instincts as to how we think we ought to play them. We look at the curve of the bridge and assume that we will need to make a downward arc, but it is actually the other way around.

### Arcs and Ellipses

Try both methods (both arcs) and notice the difference in the sound. When we use the bow arm in a counterclockwise arc (like 8 to 5 on the clock) the strings will resonate vibrantly. When we move the bow clockwise (like from 11 to 3 on the clock) the notes are separate and don't continue to ring.

Playing each chord multiple times without hesitating will help you find the smooth path. Play a series of DOWN-bow chords with your bow arm creating a circular motion, a counterclockwise ellipse. You are touching down somewhere around 7 o'clock while continuing to move the arm. Let your arm make the entire ellipse in a smooth, relaxed way.

### Begin on the far side

The other trick to keep in mind is that the bow needs to arrive on the string from the far side of the violin. Just like an airplane coming in for a landing, you want it to touch down in a smooth way. No helicopter landings for this!

To convince your arm of how far over you need to go to come in for a smooth landing, practice reaching your bow hand over the violin so that your hand is all the way to the other side of the bridge and strings. You can also practice this motion without the violin and bow. Throw your right wrist over your left shoulder.

## SPICCATO and BOUNCING BOWS

The violin bow is designed to have elasticity and flexibility. Each bow is different, so it takes some getting acquainted. When we play, the bow becomes an extension of our own arm, so when we get a new bow it may feel like a baby discovering what his hands, arms and legs can do.

The closest thing I know of to the bouncing bow strokes is dribbling a basketball. It is a combination of letting the bow bounce in its own natural way, and controlling it to do so in the way that you want it to.

### EXERCISE:
### Exploring the Bouncing Characteristics of Your Bow

#### 1. Dropping
Let the bow drop down on the string in just one place. Don't control it at all. Just see what the bow does naturally.

• Do this in different parts of the bow to see how it acts differently.

• Tighten and loosen the bow to see how that affects it.

• Drop it from different heights

This is like just letting a basketball drop without doing anything else to it.

## 2. Drop and pull

Drop the bow onto the string in a way that it bounces nicely (see above to find this out), then as it begins to bounce, pull the bow a bit (DOWN bow). Only allow the bow to bounce five times before pulling it off so it does not bounce any more.

## 3. Four DOWN-bounces, one UP

Gain more control over the bouncing by creating a consistent set of four 16th notes rhythm on the DOWN stroke followed by one UP-bow bounce. This will make it two beats. The 16ths on the first beat. The UP-bow bounce on the second beat.

## 4. Triplet DOWN-bounces, one UP.

Create a consistent triplet rhythm on the DOWN-stroke bounces followed by one UP-bow bounce. This will be two beats. The triplets on the first beat. The UP-bow bounce on the second beat.

## 5. Duplets

Two DOWNS and one UP.

## 6. DOWN-UP-DOWN-UP... Even bounces

Find one area of the bow where you can produce a series of DOWN-UP's (one of each) bouncing evenly.

Get good at it. Then expand to other areas of the bow and other speeds of bouncing bows. You will find that for each part of the bow there is one speed that the bow most wants to bounce in.

**The important thing is to first get acquainted with what your bow will do for you naturally,** instead of trying to make all those bouncing motions yourself.

That would be like trying to teach a horse to trot. The horseman can expand what the horse does naturally by working on refining or extending the horse's natural movements, but there is no need to teach the horse something he already does naturally.

## OTHER BOWINGS THAT LEAVE THE STRING

Once you and your bow have become well acquainted, and you know what you can do together with the bouncing bows above, you can add additional skills where you control the bounce of the bow (with more or less bounce), depending on the type of sound that you want.

## MORE BOWING TOPICS:

*String Crossings*, pages 63, 65-67.
*Equalizing Bow Distribution and Sound Quality*, pages 74-76.
*Developing A Rich Tone*, pages 66 and 74-76.

---

### A Better-Quality Bow

One of my teachers used to point out that **your bow should be of a higher quality than your violin**. If it isn't, you won't get the full range out of the instrument.

Better to invest in a good bow and get 100% out of what your violin can give you, than to have an expensive instrument and an inferior bow that only gives you half of what is there.

# IMPROVING INTONATION

## *It's all about relationships.*

### Different tunings

Even though we use a basic pitch range to describe each note, there is no absolute. It is always a relationship. If you play with a piano tuned to A-440 then that will be the basis that you use for playing *in tune*. If you are in an orchestra that plays with A-443, you will be playing all your notes higher. If you play in a cathedral and the organ is tuned much lower, you will have to tune your instrument down to match that.

### The weakest one or least flexible one wins

So intonation is always a relationship game. And the person who sets it will be the least capable of the players or least flexible of the instruments.

The pianist cannot change the pitch of the note she plays, so you, as a string player will have to adjust. If the cellist is not very advanced, you will have to adjust to him – even if he is wrong – if you want your notes to sound good. If you play an outdoor concert with wind players whose instruments go higher and higher as they get warmer, you will have to adjust to that, too.

The more flexible instruments and the more advanced players are the ones who end up having to adjust in a performance. In a rehearsal you may try to influence the less advanced players by playing your own notes with more determination, but when it comes to a performance, the lot will go to them.

### Tuning Double Stops, Just Intonation

Within our own instruments we need to adjust to the open strings when playing double stops. For example the B in 1st position on the A string will be played in a slightly different place if playing it as a double stop with the open E string (perfect fourth) or with the open D string (major 6th).

For more information about this, look up "tempered tuning" and "just intonation." See also page 73.

---

## Intonation – Adult Beginners

With adult beginners, their ability to hear if the notes are in tune becomes more refined as their violin skills develop. It almost seems to be like a muscle that gets stronger. So for those of you who are just starting out as adult beginners, you **will** develop a better ear as you continue to play, even if you don't just naturally have a good ear.

---

### More about IMPROVING INTONATION:

- Chapter 1, Improving Your Intonation, page 6-8.
- Chapter 4, Sing the Intervals & Knowing the sound of the next note, page 33.
- Chapter 6, Just One Note Out of Tune & A Series of Notes which are difficult to play in tune, pages 68-70.
- Chapter 6, Double Stop Fingerings, pages 70-73.
- Chapter 8, Big Shifts, pages 94-97.
- Finger Spacings/Relationships, pages 7, 121-124.
- Index of Topics, LEFT HAND, page 254-255.

# FINGER SPACINGS / RELATIONSHIPS

### *Getting "there" from "here"*

Creating reliability with the left hand for good dependable intonation is about learning the relationships and distances between the fingers. In the same way that your legs learn the spacings of the steps leading up to your front door, or the steps inside your house, you want your fingers to know the spacings from note to note in each position.

When reaching across strings, the finger spacings will feel different, even if it is a whole step from the 1st to 2nd finger in the 1st position. If it is from E (on D) to F# (on D) or E (on D) to C# (on A), it is a slightly different feeling in the fingers.

### *Block Fingering & Double Stops*

It is because of the importance of training these *finger relationships* that most teachers start beginning students with what is called "block fingering." As the player goes up the scale the fingers remain down (continuing to press down on the strings) even though this no longer has any effect on the sound. When playing a descending scale, all three fingers are put down on the fingerboard before playing the third finger.

Later, when the fingers are trained, they only hover close to the string and do not actually press down unless needed.

As players become more advanced, they practice double stops to train the finger relationships. More about how to practice these in Chapter 6, *Effective Strategies*, Double Stop Fingerings, pages 71-73.

## SCALES, ARPEGGIOS & THIRDS

Practicing scales, arpeggios and thirds are the most common ways to teach our fingers the relationships we will meet most often in the music we play.

It is important to remember that the finger memory that you want to have is a physical thing. Your mind should know the finger pattern on each string for each key, but the exact spacings will be remembered by the **muscle memory** in your fingers.

See more: pages 21, 32-33, 68-70, 121.

## LEARNING TO SHIFT
### *Moving from one position to another*

Which is easier – driving to a destination you are not very familiar with or driving home? Driving home, of course.

The same concept applies when learning to easily shift from one position to another. It is most comfortable and easiest when we are familiar with the destination we are moving to. The worst thing is to set off without knowing exactly where we are going.

---

The most important thing for shifting is:

### KNOW WHERE YOU ARE GOING

Always establish familiarity and comfort with your destination position first.

---

## Example: SHIFTING from 1st to 3rd POSITION

Let's imagine you have only learned to play in the 1st position, and now you want to shift to the 3rd position.

### 1. Get acquainted with your destination first

Start off with your hand in 3rd position (**that includes your thumb!**). Learn where the notes of the scale are in that position. Play some simple melodies by ear to get used to the new finger-spacings (narrower the higher you go).

Beethoven's *Ode to Joy* is a good one because of the stepwise motion. *Joy to the World* is just a descending scale. *The 1st Noel* is almost all stepwise motion, so that is an easy one, too. You can use *Amazing Grace* to help with the arpeggios.

### 2. Notice your surroundings

As you get more accustomed to playing the notes in the 3rd position, make note of how your left hand and arm feel when you are there. Notice how close you are to the edge of the violin and the curve in the neck where it fits into the body of the violin. Move your wrist in and out to check the distance.

> **Note:** Be sure that your whole hand is in 3rd position. It should feel just as comfortable and free as when you play in 1st position and may even feel a bit easier.

### 3. From 3rd position go down to 1st and immediately back to 3rd.

Using the metronome to insure that you move with the grace of an accomplished dancer – smoothly and reliably – play two long notes in 3rd position, then two short notes, one in 3rd then shift down to 1st, and immediately back to 3rd (to the same place that you began) for another long note.

Using the 1st finger in the 3rd position on the A string play:

D – D – D B D –

The D's are half notes (two metronome clicks). D and B (DB) are two quarter notes. The last D is another half note.

### 4. You have just shifted easily between 1st and 3rd position.

Enjoy how easy that was. Repeat it a number of times so that your arm and hand will feel more and more secure with it. Just let your arm find the easiest, smoothest way to go back and forth.

If it becomes unreliable, go back to Step 1.

### 5. Do step #3 with the 2nd and 3rd fingers.

2nd finger: E – E – E C# E –

3rd finger: F# – F# – F# D F# –

**This same system can be applied to moving to/from any position.**

## More Strategies for Improving the LEFT HAND

DOUBLE STOPS: pages 70-73, 120-121.

INTONATION: pages 119-124.

LEFT HAND: pages 254-255

RAPID FINGERING:
• Muscle Movements, "The Paganini Practicing Technique,"
   page 34.
• "I Can't Play It Fast Enough," pages 45-48.
• Speed Up the Fingers, page 62-64, 93-94.
• The Dounis Exercises to Improve Left Hand Facility, page 64.
• Simplifying Difficult Passages to be able to learn them faster,
   pages 83-87.

SHIFTING: pages 85, 94-97, 122-124, 130, 154.

VIBRATO: pages 127-137.

◆◆◆◆◆◆◆◆◆◆◆◆◆◆◆◆◆◆◆◆◆◆◆◆◆◆◆◆◆◆◆◆◆◆◆◆◆

# Improving Life-Skills

It is nice to think that as we get older we also get wiser, but what are the *Life-Skills* that enable us to handle life in a more skillful way? Is it possible to attain more mastery and competence in life in the same way that we can on the violin?

I would say, yes. But in the same way that understanding the mechanics of doing vibrato does not automatically give us the skill of playing with a pleasing vibrato, the *Life-Skills* are developed by doing them, finding what works for us and then getting better at it by doing it a lot.

### Components of the process:

1. An honest **evaluation** of where you are, what is working well and what is not.

2. Getting **clear on what you want** to do better.

3. Some sort of idea or **vision of what that *better* would be like** – what it would look like, feel like, sound like and act like.

4. Create a **good strategy** to accomplish that goal, and possibly find a teacher or mentor to help with guidance and support.

5. **Trying it out and acknowledging what worked and what did not**. What got you closer to the goal and what did not?

6. **Repetition**. Doing it so many times that you do it even when you are not fully conscious and able to purposefully choose to do the right thing. Integrate it so completely, that it becomes your natural response to situations, a habit.

◆◆◆◆◆◆◆◆◆◆◆◆◆◆◆◆◆◆◆◆◆◆◆◆◆◆◆◆◆◆◆◆

# CHAPTER ELEVEN

# Vibrato

### *What makes the sound when you play the violin?*

1. The bow pulls on the string and gets it vibrating.

2. The vibration of the string moves down into the bridge.

3. The feet of the bridge fit snugly on the top of the violin. When the bridge vibrates, the feet send that vibration into the violin top.

4. Inside the violin the sound post is wedged between the top and the back of the violin. Ideally, the top and bottom of the sound post fit snugly to the curves of the top and back of the violin. When the top vibrates, the sound post picks up that vibration.

5. The sound post sends the vibration into the back of the violin.

6. Meanwhile, the bass bar has communicated the vibration from the area of the top near the bridge all the way out beneath the fingerboard to the rest of the top.

7. And voila! A wonderful resonance that can charm, delight, and communicate has been created.

If at any point along the way this vibration is subdued or inhibited in some way, the sound is no longer so vibrant. A good example is when we put something on the bridge that squeezes it so the vibration is inhibited a bit. What we then have is a muted violin sound.

*It is good to think of the vibrato in the same way:*

### *A Vibration*
### *Moving Through Multiple Components*

To get the maximum vibration, EVERY component needs to be flexible and free. If there is stiffness anywhere, if some part is not able to move freely, the vibration will be muted, the vibrato will be choked.

## VIBRATO – KEY COMPONENTS

The optimum is when your *whole body* is flexible enough that the vibration can flow freely through it, but most important is to have flexibility and capability in these key components:

• Left Arm
• Left Wrist
• Left Hand Fingers
and added to those,
• A Clear Desire for a particular Vibrato Sound

If you are learning vibrato for the first time as an adult, it is particularly important to work with each of these components. Younger people will tend to use their bodies in larger muscle groups, whereas as we get older the muscles tend to work more independently.

## ARM

### *Begin With the Heaviest Component*

Everyone has probably heard about the example of the three sizes of stones being placed in a jar. If the large stones are put in first, there is still room for the smaller stones, but if the smallest ones are put in first, the larger stones don't fit.

With the vibrato, it is best to start by getting the largest, heaviest part of the system working first, and then to refine it with the smaller ones. It is the same idea as the way a sculptor carves a piece of stone. They make the rough shape first and then keep refining it with more and more detail.

---

### IN muscles are stronger than OUT muscles

The muscles that are used to bring our hands toward our mouths are much stronger than the muscles that move our hands in an outward motion (we started reaching to eat things VERY early in our lives!). That means that an OUT-motion will always need more training and repetitions than an IN-motion.

The most important thing is **to achieve a *regular* oscillation.** So this difference between the ease of the IN motion and OUT motion needs to be equalized.

Think of how a nice smooth sine wave looks, and make it your aim to have the oscillations as even as that.

---

## EXERCISE TO DEVELOP AN ARM VIBRATO

### 1. Forearm motion, opening and closing the elbow

You can start to gain some facility with the arm motion by using a shaker, or tapping your knuckles on something (soft). Both of these methods will give you a sound, and that will help you monitor if you are getting a regular oscillation. For tapping your knuckles, it is the OUT-motion that you want to train; the taps are "out-out-out..."

### 2. Learn the direction of the string.

The lucky thing about learning the vibrato motion is that it is the same muscles and **the same direction as shifting** up and down the string from 1st position to the upper positions.

However, the pathway up and down the string is not a natural direction for our arms to move, so your arm needs to learn that pathway by moving back and forth, up and down the string, many times.

### Sliding your hand up and down the string

Go all the way between 4th position down to 1st, and do the motion with a definite rhythm. Your arm moves OUT-OUT...

Even though the vibrato will eventually be a small fluctuation, what you are doing is teaching your arm the proper *direction*. If you don't, it will very likely tend to wiggle sideways and not move in the direction of the string. You don't want the vibrato going sideways. It is not the same as the way a guitarist gets vibrato.

**Do the sliding up and down the string with rhythm**

You want the sliding to be smooth, graceful and controlled. By introducing rhythm you will find the smoothest way to move your arm, without the path being like a bumpy road. No stops and starts, it should be a continuous motion, like tracing an ellipse. There is actually a very flat ellipse that is happening, but it is the up-down one, not sideways.

**Be sure that the motion is in your *forearm.***

You don't want your elbow pulling in towards your ribs. The motion is in the opening and closing of your elbow (although you do not want any part of your body to be locked either, so the upper arm does move a bit).

## 3. Make the motion smaller

As your forearm gets more and more accustomed to the direction up and down the string, you can begin to make the fluctuation smaller. Be sure to keep the motion smooth and even (*regular* oscillations). Eventually the arm moves while the finger stays on one note.

---

**Caution:** When you start doing smaller motions, if your muscles tighten up, stop. Go back to the big motion again. Cramping is the opposite of what you want.

---

## Arm Vibrato Only

If you only use your arm to do the vibrato, and the rest of your hand, wrist and fingers are just flexible, you can already have a fairly pleasing sounding vibrato, especially on the low notes.

---

## For a Warmer Sound

If you already have a vibrato, but it does not have the warmth that you would like, the circular rotation exercise is a good one to give you that.

## WRIST
### *Refine Your Vibrato and Give It Warmth*

Once your forearm is working well – it is steady and reliable and the vibrato sounds decent – you can begin to refine your vibrato by developing some skill in your wrist.

Whereas the *arm motion* is back and forth in the direction of the string with a very slight ellipse up and down, the *wrist motion* is an ellipse with the direction being as though you drew a circle on the fingerboard.

To the eye it will look like the wrist is going forward and back, but the rotation of the ellipse will produce a warm, rich vibrato.

If you only bend the wrist forward and back (without the arm motion), the vibrato will sound like the unduly wide vibrato of an elderly soprano.

## EXERCISE to "WAKE UP" THE MUSCLES IN YOUR WRIST, the Flexibility Which Produces Warmth in your Vibrato

**1.** Start with one finger at a time on the A string in 1st position. This is done without bowing, no sound.

**2. Slowly – very slowly! – rotate your finger so that the knuckle describes a circle.** Begin with your knuckle flat, then rotate towards the left (as you look down the fingerboard) as your knuckle moves to a steeper angle. Then back around towards the right as it flattens again. Note that the finger does not move to another note, just rotates around one note.

As you do this. your wrist will move in and out to accommodate the movement.

• The wrist comes IN as the knuckle rotates and flattens back towards the scroll.

• The wrist goes OUT as the knuckle rotates forward bringing the finger into a steeper angle.

---

### Hint For Older or Less Flexible Players:

If for some reason you are unable to move your wrist freely but still want to get some sort of vibrato, it is worthwhile developing a finger vibrato (page 135). It will not have the breadth and warmth of the arm and wrist vibrato, but it will give you something!

**The important thing is to make it as circular as possible.**
No flat places as you move around, all curved. Also keep it VERY
slow. This is not about actually doing vibrato; it is a muscle
exercise to *enable* the wrist and fingers to do a smooth vibrato.

**3. Do this with each finger.**

**4. Play with the bow and do vibrato.**
After rotating each finger, play some long notes and do vibrato in
the way that you were accustomed to doing it before doing this
exercise. You will find that your sound is now freer and
smoother.

It is a bit like finding your balance when first riding a bicycle.
The exercise will help give you the experience of the smoother,
freer way of doing vibrato. Then as you keep having that
experience, pretty soon you'll find you can "keep your balance."

---

### "Kitty Feet" Fingers

Whenever you place your fingers on the strings you
want to be using the pads as much as possible. You
don't want to be touching on the very tip, close to the
fingernail.

One teacher described how we should put our fingers
down on the fingerboard as "making your fingers like
kitty feet."

---

## FINGERS
### *The Smallest Vibrato Motion Of All*

Low notes usually sound best with a slower oscillation, and high notes with a faster one. A cellist will use an arm vibrato much more than a violinist. The speed of the vibrato also gives a feeling of solidity (slow) or electricity (fast).

Using the finger vibrato enables you to make the fastest possible vibrato because it is the smallest motion. You will especially need this when playing in the upper positions. Your wrist and arm are not able to move as freely up there and the higher notes will call for a faster, smaller vibrato.

### EXERCISE TO DEVELOP A FINGER VIBRATO
Do this with each finger separately.

1. Place your finger on the string **using as much flesh as possible.** You may need to flatten your finger joint a bit and roll away from the tip of your finger.

2. **Press and release the finger pressure on the string.** It is a sort of pumping motion that includes flexing the joint in your finger slightly and squishing down on the pad of your finger.

Like all the exercises, it is important to do the *squishing* with rhythm. It is about developing skill and control.

## DESIRE
### *Let Your Desire Guide You, Imagine What You Want*

While the previous exercises will help your body to be able to move in such a way that vibrato is possible, **the real driving force behind any good vibrato is the DESIRE to make a particular type of sound.**

In this case, wanting something very badly is a big bonus.

Vibrato is an enhancement of the life-force vibration coming from your instrument; it is about passion, desire and expressive emotion. Having a strong desire to produce a particular sound quality will guide you like a magnet towards your goal – the vibrato sound that you want for each note.

## KNOWING THE KIND OF VIBRATO YOU WANT
### *Creating Your Ideal Vibrato "Sound Idea"*

See Chapter 4, pages 32-33, for more about the *Sound Idea* concept.

**1. Listen to different violinists playing the same piece of music.** Develop an ear for what their vibratos sound like.

Characterize their sounds so that you begin be more conscious about how you discern the types of vibratos that most appeal to you. Is it electric, like silk, yummy as chocolate? Give it a color or shape, whatever is going to make it more obvious to you.

You are developing a sound-vocabulary for the shades of vibrato color.

**2.** Before you play a note, stop and sing or **get the sound that you intend to make in your head,** *then* **play.** And as you play, keep thinking the sound you want. If the muscles in your body can do it, they will give it to you.

The sound you imagine clearly

sends out the message,

"THIS IS WHAT WE WANT!"

Your muscles will do their best

to produce it for you.

◆◆◆◆◆◆◆◆◆◆◆◆◆◆◆◆◆◆◆◆◆◆◆◆◆◆◆◆◆◆◆◆◆◆◆

*The ebook, ***Playing Violin & Viola with Vibrato*** by Ruth Shilling, gives more detail about developing a satisfying vibrato. Available through Amazon.com and other booksellers online.

# Combining Technical Expertise + Passion

The above description of learning vibrato showed both how to develop the physical ability to do vibrato (the muscle-movement skills) and ways to clarify your desire (to know more specifically what you wanted).

• If we do not have the technical aspects (the abilities and/or tools needed to be able to do something) it is not going to be possible.
• If we don't have the desire, it is unlikely we will achieve it either.

If something we are aspiring to do is not working out, we can look at whether the difficulty lies in the clarity of our desire or with a lack of the needed skills and tools.

### EXAMPLE: Acquiring the Skills Needed

Jeff has been working in an electronics store. He has a good head for business and a true desire to serve others, which results in a good rapport with customers. Many of the local small business owners come into the store and in talking with them he finds that a lot of them need to have websites but don't have the time to do it themselves. A number of them ask Jeff if he could make a website for them.

Starting a web design business that would especially cater to the local small business owners would suit Jeff very well. He can start out doing it part time while he keeps his day job. He already has customers who want his services. What is missing?

Jeff needs to learn some basic skills. Although he is quite computer savvy, he needs skills using web design software, photo editing software, video software and writing good copy. With these skills he will have what it takes to run a good web design business which will be helpful and affordable for the local small business owners in his area.

### EXAMPLE: All the Technique, But . . .

Janice wants to own her own web design business. She did extensive training and has become quite an expert in the technical skills needed to create terrific websites. So she is ready to do the work, but she doesn't have any customers.

What Janice hasn't really thought about is that doing business is about serving other people – benefitting others and in turn having those people compensate her for that benefit.

Her desire was *to make websites*, not *to be of service*. So although her desire is in the direction of having a web design business, the part about serving other people is missing.

One way that Janice could change this is to include the customers in her view of her business. Who would her ideal customers be? How would she be able to benefit them? What could she do to make it a good experience for them?

As she clarifies her enlarged vision of her website business and knows the people she most wants to serve, she begins to think of ways that she can make connections with those people. When she communicates with them, they feel that she is there to help them out, and they are glad to avail themselves of her services.

*Now it's a win-win,*
*and that is the basis of a successful business!*

♦♦♦♦♦♦♦♦♦♦♦♦♦♦♦♦♦♦♦♦♦♦♦♦♦♦♦♦♦♦♦♦♦♦♦♦♦

CHAPTER TWELVE

# Strategies for Solid Memorization

## THREE MODALITIES FOR MEMORIZATION

There are three basic modalities used for memorizing music – auditory, visual and muscle memory. Each one of us will find that one type comes to us more easily, so it is easy to depend on just that one way. However, if we combine all three of these modalities, our ability to remember something becomes much more solid. If *Association* is included, it is better yet.

### *Included in this chapter:*

1. AUDITORY MEMORY – Remembering the Sound

2. VISUAL MEMORY – Remembering the Printed Music

3. MUSCLE MEMORY – Remembering the Fingering
   and Bowing

4. Using ASSOCIATION to Aid Your Memory

See also about the importance of short **Forgetting Times**, page 110.

## 1. AUDITORY MEMORY
### *Remembering the Sound*

As musicians, many of us tend to be more sound-oriented than other people. We recognize people by the sound of their voices, and we sometimes listen more to the timbre and inflections of their voices than to the words they are saying. Their voices tell us what they are *really* thinking and feeling, so it is the sound of the voice that tells us if the words are credible or not, and what is really going on.

Likewise, when getting acquainted with a new piece of music, we remember the sound of it more than how the notes look on the page or which finger played each note.

### *Story: A Break in Memory When a Piece was Memorized Using Only Auditory Memory*

Derek goes out on the stage to play his first recital. He starts out just fine, but suddenly loses it and needs to stop.

The only way he can get it back is to go all the way back to the beginning and start over. It is as though the audio recording "ribbon" inside his head was cut. Once that stream is broken, he is left adrift and completely lost.

---

If, along with the sound memory, Derek had also developed a visual and muscle memory of the piece, he would have been able to access those other ways of remembering and continue, maybe just moving forward to the next section.

### *"I can't memorize music."*
Sometimes new students will come for lessons and say that they cannot memorize music. What this usually really means is that they do not yet have good *AUDITORY memory.*

These students will still be able to memorize music if they use their visual and muscle memory.

### *Developing a memory for sound*
They can also develop their auditory memory by choosing one piece of music and listening to it hundreds of times. Eventually they will remember the succession of sounds that make up that piece. Once they have memorized the sound of one piece, they will then more readily memorize others.

### *1,000 Repetitions*
**Dr. Shinichi Suzuki** found this to be true when he taught young children haiku. He found that every child, even those with difficulty learning, were able to remember a haiku after **1,000 repetitions**. After memorizing the first one, they needed far fewer repetitions to memorize the next one. Soon the children could remember a new haiku after only hearing it a few times. They had developed *the ability to remember* by learning the first few haiku.

The reason most people think they are not capable of remembering is that they have never invested in the first 1,000 repetitions.

## Developing a *"Sound Memory"* of a New Piece

**A *Sound Memory* of a new piece is developed by:**
- **Hearing it many times**
- **Focusing on it deeply and completely**

### Repetition

Building on what he had learned from teaching the children haiku, Dr. Suzuki utilized repetition to achieve auditory memory in his *Suzuki Violin Method*. He referred to it as the "mother tongue method." Students listen to recordings of the pieces they will play many times before learning to play them. That way an *inner recording* is already embedded in their minds before they attempt to play each piece. When the kids learn this way, they are able to play pieces that are much more advanced and complex than if they were learning those pieces by reading.

### Heightened Focus

When something has a big impact on us, our senses go on high alert and the experience makes a profound imprint in our memories. Advertisers have studied ways to do this because they want the audience to remember the product they are selling. Some ways to impact people are: sudden sounds, rapid motion, and/or something with emotional impact, like basic desires, cravings or fears. These methods are not something you are likely to be using when you are memorizing a new piece of music, however if a piece of music deeply moves you or impresses you in some way, you will remember it much better.

## SPEEDING UP YOUR SOUND-MEMORIZATION

To maximize your results, use both conscious and subconscious learning methods.

### CONSCIOUS LEARNING METHODS -- *Active listening*

**• Listen giving it your undivided attention.**
Stop doing anything else and just listen to the music. See if you can pick out the main melodies and the form of the piece. Notice which parts you like the most. Look forward to hearing them as they come up in the piece. Focus only on listening and try not to let your thoughts stray to anything else. If possible, rewind or move back to an early place in the piece each time you realize that you have lost your focus.

**• Follow the printed music as you listen.**
Sit with the printed music and follow along while you listen. Tapping the rhythms on the notes as they go by will bring added benefits. Singing along as you listen to a recording is also a big help.

See also:
*Preparing your Orchestra Music More Effectively, Page 26*
*Tapping, Active Listening, page 152.*

**• Sing it back.**
When learning a short section, listen to it and then try to sing what you just heard.

## SUBCONSCIOUS LEARNING -- *Passive Listening*
- IN MOTION
- AT REST

### Entering a Receptive-Learning State
There are a number of ways to enter into an enhanced, learning-receptive state. People enter into states of light-trance a number of times each day without even being consciously aware of it. Did you ever find you missed an exit on the highway, or looked down at your watch and wondered where the time went?

People are different when it comes to what helps them relax. Some people are more relaxed when they are moving, others when they are not.

### *Passive Listening* – IN MOTION
If you relax more easily when you are in motion, below are some suggestions. It works particularly well if the activity you are involved in is repetitive or relaxing. It also helps if there is a quiet atmosphere around you.

### In the Background
Set up a recording of your piece to play repeatedly. When we used tape recorders, we could get endless-loop cassettes for this purpose. Perhaps you can make a CD or DVD with the same piece playing repeatedly or set an auto-repeat function on your mobile device.

### As the recording of your piece plays repeatedly:
- Go about doing your daily chores or housework
- Use an exercise bike, treadmill or a rowing machine
- Do yoga or Tai Chi
- Go out for a walk, listening on your mobile device

## *Passive Listening* – AT REST

If you feel more relaxed and at ease when you are sitting or lying down, here are two suggestions for entering a light-trance state where you will learn easily and quickly.

For both suggestions below, set up a recording of your piece to play repeatedly while you relax into a highly receptive state of accelerated learning.

### • Relaxation Techniques:

Possibilities: taking a hot bath, sitting outdoors and watching the wind in the trees, lying in a hammock, swaying on a porch swing, rocking in a rocking chair. To go deeper you can stare at the ceiling, and when your eyes tire, let them close. There are also a number of different relaxation methods that involve using the breath.

### • Here are a few calming breath methods:

1. Continue breathing normally without attempting to change it in any way, and put your attention on the sensations as the air comes in and out of your body.

2. Count IN-2-3-4, OUT-2-3-4-5-6, rest, rest, IN-2-3-4....

3. As above with the IN through your nose and OUT through your mouth, like gently blowing out a candle.

4. Breath IN with eyes closed, OUT with eyes open, releasing any busy thoughts.

### • Hypnosis Recordings are available for accelerated learning and improved performance. Choose one that does not have background music so you can listen to your own music at the same time.

## 2. VISUAL MEMORY
### *Remembering the Printed Music*

Some people are gifted with what is called *photographic memory*. When they read something or look at something closely a visual imprint is made in their memory. Once they have read a certain passage, they can later recall that passage by simply "reading it" in their minds.

Most people have this ability to a lesser extent and use it without even thinking about it.

*Example:* Many of us use *visual memory* when we are driving and remembering where to turn. We look for landmarks and then remember how things will look when we turn left or right.

*Example:* If you read something in a book and later you are trying to remember where it was, you may know what part of the page it was written on.

Note: Some people visualize things by "knowing" what is in their mind's eye, rather than actually seeing it as a picture in their minds.

## BENEFITS OF VISUAL MEMORY

### Knowing where you are in the piece
Visual memory can be like a map that shows us where we are in a piece of music. As we play, we can see where we are on the page and what comes next.

For example when playing a piece in Rondo form (ABACA, ABACABA or similar), the "A" section repeats a number of times throughout the piece. If we have a visual memory of where we are on the page, we know which "A" section we are playing. If we have only a *sound memory* of the piece, we may play the wrong section after one of the "A" sections.

### Getting back in if you miss something

Another advantage is that you will remember how each section starts and be able to move ahead to it, getting back in if you miss something in the preceding section. If you make a mistake, the audience wants you to keep on going. They do not want to have to watch you start all over again from the beginning.

## DEVELOPING A VISUAL MEMORY OF A PIECE
### Here are two methods.

#### • Write Out the Notes
One highly effective method (which is, unfortunately, also pretty toilsome) is to sit and write out the notes of a passage you want to memorize. If you can do this, you will have a clear memory of what the notes are.

#### • Seeing Where You Are In the Music
Another method, and one that works very well as an adjunct to using *sound memory* and *muscle memory*, is to work with seeing where you are in the music. This can be done easily and fairly quickly.

Excellent results are guaranteed if you just go through the steps methodically (see next page).

## *Steps to Seeing Where You Are in the Music*

**1.** Put the metronome on at a comfortable speed. Play the section or piece that you want to memorize. Play it 3 times in a row correctly and with ease.

**2.** Step back about a foot and play it again. **Be sure to keep your eyes on the music as you play,** even if you remember how it goes.

**3.** Once you can play it easily 3 times in a row, step back farther and play it again.

**4.** Repeat, until the music is too far away for you to actually read the notes. At this point you will be seeing where you are in the piece and remembering what is within the section you are playing.

**While doing this process, it is important to:**

**• Play with ease.**
Never play in such a way that you tense up or strain. If you have trouble, just move forward again and play it until it becomes more solid.

**• Maintain accuracy in rhythm.**
As we get to know a piece better, it is easy to start speeding up unintentionally. If you want to play faster, move the metronome up but keep everything rhythmically accurate.

**• Keep your eyes on the place you are playing.**
It is easy to stop actually looking at the notes as you begin to remember it, but for training the visual memory, it is important to keep your eyes following your location on the page of music.

## VARIATIONS on this method:

• If you wear glasses for distance, you can just take your glasses off.

• If you have access to a copy machine or scanner, make a series of copies in smaller versions – 90%, 80%, 70%, etc. This is especially helpful if you don't have enough room to move back far enough from the music stand. Pianists can use this method, too.

## 3. MUSCLE MEMORY
### Remembering the Fingering & Bowing

The most effective way to develop muscle memory is to play a piece hundreds of times. When our bodies have done something hundreds or thousands of times, we no longer need to guide it with our minds. The body remembers and just does it without our needing to think about it.

### If your mind loses focus for a few seconds
Muscle memory can be a real blessing if we are performing and for a moment, our concentration drops or we get distracted. If we have played the piece enough times, the fingers and bow continue playing even without our mental focus.

### Fast notes
Another time the muscle memory is particularly needed is when the notes are too fast for us to think of and plan each one individually. We can *program them into the hand*, so to speak, and then just flip the switch for that passage.

### *Developing MUSCLE MEMORY More Quickly*

Below are some ways to promote the muscle-memory learning. These will speed up the learning and reduce the number of times needed to instill this type of memory.

- Tapping
- Finger Patterns
- The First Note of a Phrase or Section

### • *Tapping*

Go through your piece tapping the rhythms with a pencil held in your right hand (bow hand). Next, go through again, this time tapping with the *fingers* on the left hand. This will help your body to remember the rhythms. See also pages 26, 32, and 145.

### • *Finger Patterns*

Knowing the whole finger pattern (the spacings of all four fingers) will help you see the fingerings in groupings, rather than just individually.

*EXAMPLE*: If you are going to play a 2-octave scale all in one position, practice putting all four fingers down in the correct relationships, one string at a time. Know the patterns of whole steps and half steps for each string.

By putting all four fingers down at once as a unit, you will imprint your muscle memory with that *pattern* as a unit. It is now like a word, instead a series of random letters.

It is similar to how a ballet dancer has 1st position, 2nd position, etc. Each leg and arm is not remembered separately. The 1st position includes both arms and both legs and is remembered as one pose. You want the finger-memory to be that way, too – one *pattern-unit* on each string.

## • *The First Note of a Phrase or Section*

Creating a clear memory of how we start each phrase and section is an essential part of having a solid memory of the piece. Learn both the bowing and fingering.

### *For the first-note BOWINGS:*

• Is it an UP bow or DOWN bow?

• What is the best place to start that note – tip, middle, frog?

• Will it be a fast bow or slow bow? This will also affect how close you will play to the bridge.

### *For the first-note FINGERINGS:*

• Where is that note on the fingerboard?

• Which finger do you play that note with?

• What is the name of the note?

• Which position are you in?

• What is the relationship of that note to both the preceding note and following note?

**Test yourself on each starting note.**

Go through the piece playing only the 1st note of every large section in the piece.

Then go through each section and test yourself that you can play the first note of every phrase in that section. **Particularly important are the notes immediately after a rest.**

Being able to start anywhere is especially important when we are performing. If something goes wrong, we can start at the beginning of the next phrase. Mid-phrase is even better.

## Being Able to Start Anywhere in the Piece

One common mistake made by students and amateurs is to always start at the beginning of a piece.

This is like the woman who insisted that the only way to find a letter in the alphabet was to start at the very beginning of the Alphabet Song and sing all the way through until she reached the right letter.

I worked in a library and was assigned the job of shelving books which were in alphabetical order by author. I learned the alphabet in sections and where each section fit. If every time I shelved a book, I had to sing from the beginning of the Alphabet Song for every letter in the author's name, I never would have gotten my work done.

**Always starting at the beginning
wastes a lot of time.**

## SHIFTS

As well as knowing all the beginning notes, you also want to be very sure of the notes you are shifting to when you change positions. The same criteria that are listed above for the starting-notes also apply to the shifting-notes. There is more about shifting on pages 94-97, 122-124, and 130.

## 4. USING ASSOCIATION to AID YOUR MEMORY

It is easier to remember things we are already familiar with. If we see something as resembling something familiar, it is easier to remember.

### Attaching something known to something new

We can attach something we have already learned to something new. If my sister's name is Barbara and I meet someone new named Barbara, I can think, "Oh, she has the same name as my sister." Making that association will make it much more likely that I will remember her name.

### Looking for patterns we already know

In music when we see scales or arpeggios that we already know, we can think of them like words that fit into the whole, instead of a series of individual letters.

When a beginning student first learns *Twinkle, Twinkle Little Star* and later learns *May Song*, realizing that the form of both songs is the same can make it much easier to remember what is coming up. "Oh, it is the same as the "Twinkle Sandwich – bread-cheese-cheese-bread" (the "A-b-b-A" form).

*EXAMPLES:*

### *"Pepperoni Pizza"*— four 16th notes followed by two 8ths

For a student who has learned using the Suzuki method, he might see the first movement of the Bach Double violin concerto as beginning with a scale, then jumping to the octave, and played with the "Pepperoni Pizza" rhythm. He is just putting a series of notes he already knows to a rhythm he already knows.

**Mississippi Reel**

The *Mississippi Reel* starts out with the rhythm "Pepperoni Pepperoni Pepperoni Pizza." Each "Pepperoni" is a descending scale. The "Pizza" is an octave. The second line is the same finger pattern on the D string, except the "Pizza" is two open A's. Seeing it this way makes it easy to learn that piece quickly.

◆◆◆◆◆◆◆◆◆◆◆◆◆◆◆◆◆◆◆◆◆◆◆◆◆◆◆◆◆◆◆◆

# Effective Memorization
# for
# Daily Life

When studying for tests, students often need to memorize a series of words, dates, or concepts. Violin students can use the skills they learn on the violin to help them be high academic achievers as well.

Here are a few methods that can be helpful, especially for those who have studied music. Just as with the violin, the most potent way to memorize is to combine the three modalities – Sound+Visual+Muscle memory – and add in any associations that are possible.

## *MEMORIZING THE SPELLING OF A WORD*

Suggestions using different types of memory or a combination of those:

### 1. Melodies – Auditory Memory

The alphabet song (ABCD to the tune of *Twinkle, Twinkle Little Star*) helped most of us learn the alphabet. Using a melody helps with remembering the spelling of words, too. You can use the melody of a song you already know, or you can make up a new melody.

If there are any letters that are hard to remember, sing them with some sort of **special emphasis**.

*Suggestions:*

• as a longer note

• with an accent

• as a higher note

• with a rest before singing the important letter

### 2. Visual memory

Look at the word, then close your eyes and write the word, seeing the letters in your mind.

### 3. Muscle memory

Write the word in large letters. Trace each letter with your finger. Now write the letters in the air.

### 4. Muscle memory

Write the word holding the pencil in your fist instead of the normal way. That way you will need to use your arm more intentionally.

### 5. Muscle memory

Write the word first with your dominant hand (the right hand for most people) and then with your non-dominant hand.

### 6. Visual+Muscle memory

Write the word, then trace over it with the pencil. Now close your eyes and try to trace over it again (keeping your eyes closed).

### 7. Sound+Visual+Muscle memory

Write the word while you sing or say the letters out loud. Then trace the letters with your finger while you sing the letters. Now close your eyes, sing and write the letters.

## REMEMBERING A PHONE NUMBER & STREET ADDRESS

The mother of one of my students told me how when her daughter was small, they made up a little song to help her daughter remember their phone number and street address. This is an important thing for all children to remember, and a song is a great way to do that.

## REMEMBERING DATES

Again, a phrase that rhymes is a charmer. I always remember 1492 because we learned, "Columbus sailed the ocean blue in fourteen-hundred-ninety-two." You can also use the same modes as given above for memorizing a word.

## MEMORIZING FOR MATH
### Example: Multiplication Tables

**1. Devise a clever rhythm** with which to say the sentence that you want to remember.

*EXAMPLE:* **2 X 2 = 4**
Say "two times two is FOUR, YES!" using the rhythm of four 16ths followed by two 8ths. This is the first rhythm introduced in the Suzuki Violin Method ("Pepperoni Pizza," "Mississippi Hotdog," etc.).

**2. Find something that rhymes or sounds similar.**

*EXAMPLE:* **7 X 6 = 42**
"Got a <u>heavenly</u> **mix** for **you**." (rest) "<u>Seven</u> times **six** is <u>forty</u>-**two**!"

**3. Use *sounds-like* with a visual cue and put rhythm to it.**

*EXAMPLE:* **8 X 6 = 48**
"What I <u>ate</u> has made me <u>sick</u>, wish I'd thought be<u>fore</u> I <u>ate</u>!"
"What I **8** has made me **6**, wish I'd thought be**4** I **8**!"

**4. Use rhythm and association**

*EXAMPLE:* **56 = 7 X 8**
"5, 6, 7, 8. Fifty-six is seven times eight."
This one uses association because the numbers are in consecutive order, which is familiar, already known.

◆◆◆◆◆◆◆◆◆◆◆◆◆◆◆◆◆◆◆◆◆◆◆◆◆◆◆◆◆◆◆◆◆◆

# CHAPTER THIRTEEN

# Practice Time

## Making SUCCESS a Habit!

### *Clear goals for your practice session*

Having a definite achievable goal for something you are working on sets you up to have a feeling of success and accomplishment when you achieve it.

### *Quantify Your Goals*

If the goal is just that it "sounds better," how will you know when you have reached that? If there is a way to know when the goal is achieved, the chances of getting that sweet satisfaction of accomplishment are much greater.

*EXAMPLE: I want to be able to play this passage correctly with the metronome on 120.*

### *Making SUCCESS a Habit*

No matter what it is you are practicing, the best goal is to find ways that you can do things successfully, and then to reinforce that with repetition until it happens without your needing to monitor it. The more experiences of playing-something-well you can log in, the better it is! See pages 1-5.

## A Sample PRACTICE ROUTINE

Here is a basic Practice-Time Layout that you can adapt to whatever you are presently working on.

1. **Set the Bar**, get everything working well, warm-ups.
2. **Embody a High Standard**, something you play well.
3. **Work in Progress.**
4. **All's Well the Ends Well.**

### 1. Set the Bar, get everything working well, warm-ups

Like a ballet dancer or athlete, doing some warm-ups is a good way to both wake up the muscles, and to set a high standard for the rest of the practice session. The most common way to do this is to play scales and arpeggios.

### Some of the things to cover in your warm-ups:

• A high standard of bowing. Many people start by playing some open strings.

• Accurate intonation and a good left hand position.

• Shifting exercises to engage the left arm.

• Vibrato exercises, if you are working on that.

### 2. Embody a High Standard, something you play well

Not only do we like to aim high, but if we can start off at the top of our game, it starts things off in a good way. Playing something which you already play well reminds you what your potential is and sets the standard for the rest of your practice time.

### 3. Work in Progress

Now you are ready to tackle the work of the day. This will be the bulk of your practice time.

## 4. All's Well that Ends Well

No matter what happened during the time you were working on new challenging things, it is always good to "end on a good note."

In the same way that if you have an argument or unpleasant experience with someone, it will linger in your memory each time you think of that person, the last thing you do during your practice time will linger in your subconscious until the next time you play. How much better it is if what you end your practice with is a satisfying feeling.

### *Play something you love and that you play well.*

It can be a short melody or a passage from a longer piece you particularly enjoy. No need to judge yourself. Just enjoy it – both your own skills and the strength of the music.

---

## "Bad days"

Sometimes nothing seems to be working well. The frustrations can mount as we try valiantly to get things back on track.

### *Advice: Don't leave the violin defeated.*

• Find something easy that *will* work.

• Play it in an easy tempo that is not stressful or taxing.

• Keep your practice session short.

• Then spend the rest of your practice time doing some *active listening* (see pages 145, 152).

## To be able to practice longer, take breaks

When I was an avid music student, I practiced 4-6 hours a day and then often had rehearsals in the evening. I soon discovered that if I wanted to be able to keep playing for that many hours, it was necessary to take breaks. If I practiced for 90 minutes without stopping, my muscles would tire, and I would have to stop for the day.

The strategy that worked for me was to **set a timer** for 50 minutes. Then I would take a short break before playing for another 50 minutes.

Orchestra rehearsals and performances can go on for much longer than that, but we are not playing continuously in that case, whereas when we practice we just keep going.

Another way to give your muscles a break is to **intersperse the practice time with working on the music without playing**. Active listening, singing the phrases, and imagining the muscle movements, creating your *Sound Idea* are all good uses of the resting times (page 32-34, 152).

## INCORPORATING PRACTICE TIME
### into Your Daily Life

During my many years of teaching, I have noticed that the people who are most able to get in regular practice times and make steady progress are the people who keep a consistent schedule in their lives in general. People who are well meaning, but have different commitments each day, have a lot of trouble practicing consistently.

The most tried and true method is to incorporate the practicing into an already existing routine. The best is something that happens at the same time each day (like eating).

*EXAMPLE*: When a child gets home from school, she has a snack and then does her practicing.

*EXAMPLE*: A retired adult who has lots of varied activities has a routine of each morning after breakfast having his coffee while reading the morning paper, and then practicing before doing anything else.

*EXAMPLE*: A child has a lot of after school activities. Both parents work and there is a constant juggling of schedules to get everyone to their different activities. In addition, there is always a lot of homework that is assigned.

*Solution:* Do the practicing in the morning before school. If the child needs to leave for school very early, make it a prescribed 15-minute routine that happens every day in the morning. Then make a longer routine for the afternoons or evenings. If the practice times later in the day get missed, at least there is the continuity of the morning slots.

*Whenever possible, find an activity that is regular and piggyback the practice time onto that.*

## Shortest Forgetting Time = Most Rapid Learning
See the importance of having the shortest *Forgetting Times* between practice sessions, page 110.

◆◆◆◆◆◆◆◆◆◆◆◆◆◆◆◆◆◆◆◆◆◆◆◆◆◆◆◆◆◆◆◆◆◆

# Time Management

There are a lot of different approaches to time management. People have such different personalities that what works for one person may not work for someone else at all. Here is a suggestion that may or may not apply to your personality type.

## GETTING THE "DRAG-TASKS" DONE
### *Assigning Them a New Meaning and Relevance*

### Inspired Action

Have you ever noticed that when you are enthused about something and you are doing it, the time flies, you have vast amounts of energy and you can accomplish massive amounts of work?

On the other hand, a task that feels like "a drag" might only take 10-15 minutes, but days and days can go by and it never seems to get done.

### Smaller Tasks Supporting Over-Arching Goals

One way to use the momentum of inspired action is to establish clear life goals. Once we have the over-arching goal established – and it should be **something you feel a true desire for** – then the activities of each day are slotted into how they *support* achieving those goals.

When we see the mundane activities that have to be done, as moving us towards what we *want*, it is easier to let the momentum of the overall goal carry us through the less exciting ones.

## EXAMPLE: Housework as Thinking Time

Janice hated doing housework. It was boring, and it made her feel worthless. She felt it was demeaning that she needed to spend her time doing it.

When she got the idea to start a new project (goal) she reassigned the housework time to being **thinking time**. While she was doing the dishes or vacuuming, she let that work get done on automatic pilot, and she used it as time to run different scenarios in her head for her new project.

She was even surprised to notice that the more boring and "mindless" the tasks were, the more likely she was to get inspired ideas and solutions to problems that she otherwise would not figure out.

*Clear Goals open the way*
*to Inspired Action.*

◆◆◆◆◆◆◆◆◆◆◆◆◆◆◆◆◆◆◆◆◆◆◆◆◆◆◆◆◆◆◆◆◆◆◆◆◆◆◆

# CHAPTER FOURTEEN

# Using Circumstances to Our Advantage

If we think to do it, we can often find ways to use our present circumstances to our advantage. Even things which we might at first think are a detriment can often be used to help us, or improve things for us.

*EXAMPLES:*

• MOVING TO A BIGGER VIOLIN
• AFTER TAKING A BREAK FROM THE VIOLIN
• A NEW PIECE OF MUSIC

---

### A Good Time to Move to a Larger Sized Violin

Because the student will need to learn new finger spacings on a larger instrument, making that switch is easiest when there has been a break in practicing. After a summer vacation is an ideal time to move to a larger instrument.

---

## MOVING TO A BIGGER VIOLIN

As children grow, they move from smaller to larger violins until they eventually play a full size. Switching to the next size up can be a challenge, especially for the left hand because the notes are now spaced further apart.

How can this be turned into something helpful?

**Getting a different sized violin is an ideal time to:**

• Upgrade the accuracy of the left hand fingerings

• Improve the bow tone

### • Improved intonation

When first learning to play the violin, a child may just get the notes in the general area of where they should be but not exactly in the right place on the fingerboard. Sometimes one has to celebrate that they are at least using the right finger and getting a note that is recognizably the right one, even if it is not really in tune.

When a child moves up to a larger sized violin, it is an ideal time to get more specific about where the fingers go on the fingerboard.

### • Improved bowing and tone

The larger-sized violins have more sound. This makes it a wonderful time to focus on making a much fuller, richer sound with the bow, and enjoying the satisfaction which comes with that – for both the child playing the violin, and everyone else in the house!

## AFTER TAKING A BREAK FROM THE VIOLIN

When we take some time off from playing, things can be a bit rusty when we come back to it. Our bodies forget how to do things if we stop doing them for a while. After a break you pick up the violin to play that familiar piece and your fingers and/or bow just don't seem to work anymore. How can this possibly be an advantage?

What is the problem? My body doesn't remember how to do things the way I used to.

That can be bad or good. Bad because we can't play everything at the standard we could before. Good because we *don't* play everything the way we did before. What is good about that?

We have forgotten our bad habits just as much as our skills.
We can use this to our advantage by making this a time to upgrade our technique.

### Story:
### Using a Vacation from the Violin to his Advantage

Carl first learned violin at school in the 5th grade. Because there were many kids in the class all learning to play at once, and also because the music teacher was really a guitarist, Carl never learned to hold the bow correctly. He played for two years at school with a bad bow hold.

For 7th grade he started in a new school and wanted to improve his violin playing so he could play in that school's orchestra. He started private lessons with a violin teacher (Ruth).

I helped him a lot during his first year of lessons, but Carl was unable to change his bow hold because it was so ingrained in his body memory. He learned the correct bow hold, but he still ended up holding the bow the old way when he played.

During the summer vacation, he went away to soccer camp and did not play the violin at all. In September he started with the private violin lessons again. He arrived at his first lesson without having taken the violin out of the case since the end of June.

Carl was worried I would be angry. He thought I would probably scold him for not practicing all summer. What a surprise when my response was, "OK. You haven't played for 2 months so that means your body will have forgotten a lot of how to play the violin. **Let's use this to your advantage**."

"The bad news is that you are going to have to relearn some things that you could already do last June. The good news is that you have forgotten your bad habits just as much as your skills.

"This is a perfect time for us to work on fixing your bow hold. You have a wonderful chance to really upgrade your playing by **developing that as a new habit**. This will enable you to play better than you ever have before."

And that is just what we did.

## A NEW PIECE OF MUSIC

When we are just starting to learn a piece, the disadvantage could be that we don't yet have the skills needed to play it, but there are benefits, too.

### • We are a clean slate.

If it is a piece we played earlier, we may have to *unlearn* bad habits we developed the first time we played it. With a new piece, we have not developed any misconceptions about it yet. This gives us an opportunity to learn it in the most effective and efficient way. We can capitalize on this advantage by being especially careful to learn the new piece correctly.

### • The piece can motivate us to develop new skills.

If this piece requires skills which we presently do not have, wanting to be able to play it can be a good reason to work hard to develop those new skills. That is much more fun than learning a technique without having an application for it.

◆◆◆◆◆◆◆◆◆◆◆◆◆◆◆◆◆◆◆◆◆◆◆◆◆◆◆◆◆◆◆◆◆◆◆◆

# Letting Circumstances Bring Us Benefit in Life

Things don't always go as planned or the way we wanted them to or the way we thought they would. When we are in the *SUCCESS* mode these situations become an opportunity to see how each circumstance can bring us benefit. Here is an approach that may suit you.

**The Steps:**

1. Being in Truth about *what is*.

2. Accepting that and doing any grieving that is needed.

3. A willingness to enlarge yourself and your previous ideas.

4. Reframing it in a larger context.

5. "How could this benefit me?"

6. Coming up with a new plan.

## 1. Being in Truth about *What Is*

The more we allow ourselves to see what is *really* happening, the more powerful our position. Likewise, the more we work hard to convince ourselves that things are the way we *want* them to be, the weaker and more vulnerable we are.

It's easy to want things to be a certain way and then look for reasons why that could be true, but that can end up being a trap. We get attached to our ideas about how we think things are, and it can feel like a death to let go of those ideas.

Sometimes it *is* a death – someone passes on, a relationship ends, our job is terminated... Even when it is obvious that something happened, there is a protection mechanism inside us that wants to keep us from the pain of knowing that. It can create a sort of *knowing and not knowing* state.

A friend was telling me recently that it was three years before it really hit him that his mother had died. Intellectually he knew that, but he had not really allowed it to be real for himself. It is not that he did this on purpose, it happened naturally within his subconscious.

To move forward with this process, we first need to acknowledge a situation or the circumstance for what it is.

*Examples:*
The plane is delayed.
It is raining, snowing, sweltering hot...
The electricity is out.
I got laid off from my job.
My car was totaled.
My spouse left me.
The economy is in recession.
I am no longer 35.
The stock market went down.

## 2. Accepting It and Doing any Grieving That is Needed

Often we need some time to absorb the news or grieve it, so it is good to allow the time needed to walk through it at a pace that works for us.

It is natural to go into denial when we see *what is* and we don't want it to be that way. Not allowing ourselves the time we need to absorb something will usually just get us sucked deeper into the quicksand of denial.

Depending on the severity of the situation, this stage can take a few minutes or a number of years.

## 3. A Willingness to Enlarge Yourself and Your Previous Ideas

To get out of being stuck, things often need to be enlarged in some way. If I lost my job, maybe it is time to become an employer instead of being an employee. If my car was totaled, maybe a different type of vehicle would actually suit me better. When I was 35 I was trying so hard to have people think I was this or that, now that I am older I can just relax and be myself.

### Limits & Increasing Freedom

Seeing how the old version of things was limiting us can also be helpful. If my spouse left me, maybe I will enjoy ruling my own house, having the freedom to choose my activities spontaneously without needing to check how it fits with someone else, use my vacation time in the way I always wanted to, spend time with the people I really enjoy, stay up late, sleep in, try new things.

## 4. Reframing It in a Larger Context

We can also enlarge it by seeing it in the context of our whole lives. I remember an undergraduate student who felt devastated by a lesson with her cello teacher. It helped when I pointed out that she would have a series of teachers and she would be a teacher herself someday. She would have a long, full, rich career as a cellist, and this incident would be just one tiny frame in the movie of her life.

Likewise, with a plane delay it is just one small event in the context of a life.

If you believe that God has a plan for you, the present situation can be seen as part of the God's larger plan. If you don't have that belief system, you can see how the situation can fit into your own larger plan for yourself, the bigger and better things that are coming into your life, and the direction of your desires.

The reframing process helps to loosen up the hold that the old ideas (*how things were supposed to be*) had on us.

## 5. "How could this benefit me?"

It is amazing how just asking the question and looking for an answer can help us find a new perspective. And it may not be just one answer. There may be many ways this could be a benefit. It just takes looking for them.

**Basic question:** "How can this benefit me?"
**Supportive question:** "What are my overall goals? Is there any way this could help me with any of those?"

Sometimes just putting the situation into a context that there *is* a possible benefit is all that needs to happen.

*Good questions can*
*open doorways and wider perspectives.*

## 6. Coming up with a New Plan

If we have gleaned some sort of benefit from the questioning, then how would utilizing that look? Devise a new plan.

### *Questions:*

• How could I put that into practice?

• What would be a step I could take *right now* to start putting that into practice?

## 7. Acting ⇒ Empowered Again

Taking action in the present makes the change in perspective real. Without that, it can remain as a fantasy or just an abstract idea.

Having something *happen to us* that we did not want can bring on a feeling of powerlessness. After all, we didn't want it to happen, but it still did. Choosing and then acting on a new plan brings us back into the driver's seat of our own personal power. That feels a lot better.

◆◆◆◆◆◆◆◆◆◆◆◆◆◆◆◆◆◆◆◆◆◆◆◆◆◆◆◆◆◆◆◆◆◆◆

CHAPTER FIFTEEN

# Choosing a Teacher

The burden of learning is on the student. A teacher cannot make someone learn. They can offer the students their best, but if the student does not take it in, act on it and make it his own, the teacher cannot make this happen. Some people will learn a lot from one teacher, while others will study with that same teacher and learn very little.

Each teacher has a different set of abilities and skills, as well as their own personality traits. Finding what it is that you can best learn from each teacher helps you get the most benefit from your lessons.

### Story: Wish I had known...

One of my teachers was a Naumburg Competition winner. He had been the concertmaster of the Julliard School orchestra and had received his doctorate from there. He was an outstanding musician and greatly admired.

I practiced diligently and tried to follow what he taught me, but I did not really get a lot out of my lessons with him. Other students raved about what they were learning from him. What was my problem?

The light bulb went off one day when I was no longer studying with him. I walked past his studio window and saw him playing with one of his students. He was such an inspiring player.

Then I realized that he had never played with me in any of my lessons. I had never heard him play any of the pieces I was working on. The reason was that, although he played viola in his chamber music group, his principal instrument was the violin.

He never had his viola with him during my lessons, so instead he tried to tell me in words what would help me. He was not very articulate when talking about music. It came so naturally to him that he hadn't analyzed it enough to be able to describe it very well.

If I had only figured this out when I was studying with him I could have handed him my viola and asked him to play the passage he was trying to describe. Or I could have asked that he bring his viola to the lessons and play with me. Playing along with him would have taught me a lot.

Regrettably, that is a missed opportunity. I can only hope my story will help someone else.

## DIFFERENT WAYS of TEACHING and LEARNING

- The teacher inspires the student by playing beautifully.
- The teacher demonstrates something by playing it.
- The teacher explains something to the student.
- The teacher points out where the student needs to improve, or the mistakes the student is making.
- The teacher assigns etudes and exercises that will benefit the student.
- Teacher and student play together. The student gets the feel of it by linking up with the teacher, and also notices the differences between how he and the teacher play.
There is more about *Entrainment*, pages 235-249.
- The teacher guides the student through a process that results in the student being able to play something which he could not play before. Result: an experience of *SUCCESS*!
*Example:* "I can't play it fast enough" story, pages 45-48.
- Watching your fellow students, learning by observing someone else's mistakes and triumphs.
- Listening to and watching great performers.

**Which modalities work best for you?**
For most violin students, their lessons will be a combination of the learning modalities listed above.

Which of the above modalities are the easiest ways for you to learn? Is it easiest for you to get something by just holding your focus on what you want and trying to get it? Or is it easier for you if you understand what you are doing, along with why and how it works that way? What helps you to be able to reproduce at home what you were able to do in the lesson?

## Which modalities work best for your teacher?

Which are the ways your teacher is most capable of helping you? How can you get the most from the teachers that you have access to? As in the story above, if I had figured out that playing along with that teacher would have been the best way to learn from him, I could have gotten a lot more out of those lessons. And we both would have enjoyed it more.

## The goal is that YOU can play better

Sometimes people can fall into the glamor of wanting to say that they study with someone famous or well known, sort of like owning an expensive car or home.

If you are hoping that your teacher will help you with professional connections, this may have merit. However, if you want to play your instrument better, the proof is in the effect that the teacher has on *your* playing, not on how well the teacher plays.

## Can this teacher bring me closer to my goals?

When choosing a teacher, the most important thing to consider is whether that teacher can bring you closer to your goals. The possibilities and options listed in Chapter 2, *Setting Goals,* (pages 16-17), can be a used to help evaluate what those are.

If both you and the teacher know what your goals are, it will help you both make good decisions and choices about how to use your time and where to put your focus.

### *Story: A Teacher Who Got Results*

One of my fellow students from college was a good flutist, but not outstanding. She did not pursue a professional career, but rather became a private flute teacher. She always had a full teaching load, and never lacked for students.

Why? Because every year her flute students won the top spots in the all-state orchestra and band.

So even though she was not a top-notch professional player, she knew how to get her students to the level where they wanted to be.

---

### *Best of all...*

The best teacher will get you to do things that are beyond what you thought it was possible for you to do.

> The burden of learning is on the student,
> but if a teacher can get you
> to
> SURPASS YOUR LIMITATIONS,
> you have got a good one!

◆◆◆◆◆◆◆◆◆◆◆◆◆◆◆◆◆◆◆◆◆◆◆◆◆◆◆◆◆◆◆◆◆◆◆◆

# Choosing Mentors

In the same way that the best violin teacher for each one of us is the one who has the effect of getting us to play better than we could on our own, our teachers and mentors in life can lift us up, inspire us and guide us towards being more of the person that is our best self.

Whenever I visit a church or spiritual group, I look around at the people there. What sort of an effect is this teaching or dogma having on the people who follow and practice it? It may sound good on paper or in lectures, but what is the outcome when people ascribe to it?

I hosted a tour for a group of followers of a spiritual teacher who focused on prosperity and abundance. However, the people in the group were the least generous group of people I ever worked with. That lack of generosity spoke louder than the words the teacher was speaking in his lectures.

What I look for in mentors or teachers is the effect that they have on me when I am in their presence.

### *Story: Mother Teresa Comes To Boston*

Mother Teresa was scheduled to speak at a church in Boston. At that time I did not really know much about her. I only had a vague idea of who she was, but I knew she was an outstanding human being, so I was interested to see for myself.

Two of my friends and I had planned to go together, but it was hard to coordinate with the large crowds of people. I was in a large group that waited for about an hour outside the church where she was to speak.

When she stepped out of the car and I first saw her, my heart leaped. There was a LOVE that rushed through me as pure emotion from the heart.

One my friends, a Jewish woman from Canada, managed to befriend some monks on her way there and they helped her get inside the church. When she first saw Mother Teresa she was also overwhelmed by the love that went through her. She said it was so intense that she wanted to prostrate herself and renounce all her worldly possessions (which would have been quite a few!).

My other friend, who is Chinese, could not find a parking place after dropping me off at the church, so went home and watched the event on TV. His reaction when he saw Mother Teresa was also a rush of pure heart-love.

When we got together to talk about it, we were struck by how we all reacted in a similar way, even though we were in different locations and came from different backgrounds.

*The value of a mentor or teacher is evident in the effect that they have on us.*

*Do they help us bring our best self forward?*

◆◆◆◆◆◆◆◆◆◆◆◆◆◆◆◆◆◆◆◆◆◆◆◆◆◆◆◆◆◆◆◆◆

CHAPTER SIXTEEN

# Playing in Groups

Playing music with others can be a supreme joy. It gives us a chance to participate in the richness of harmonies, to be a part of a greater whole, and to enjoy the camaraderie of other musicians.

## Some Reasons to Play Music with Other People:

- It's fun.
- It gives us richer musical opportunities – duets, trios, string quartets, violin sonatas, orchestral pieces, musicals, operas...
- Being in a group creates momentum – regular meetings, group goals and performances.
- Parent-child relationships can be strengthened.
- Other people's enthusiasm can invigorate us, and can keep us going when we might falter.
- It is an enjoyable way to socialize with other people.

## Some of the Challenges:

- Finding other people who are at a similar playing level.
- Scheduling rehearsals. People need to have similar times available to get together, and to show up reliably.
- Amenable personalities. Some groups just gel better than others. People who are overbearing, egotistical or negative can mess it up.
- Finding people who play the instruments for the literature you want to play.

## Consider yourself lucky

The challenges can make finding your perfect group pretty difficult. If you find something that meets most of what you want in a group, consider yourself lucky.

## How are they helping me fulfill my goals and desires?

Playing music with other people has the same components as other human relationships – both the joys and the frustrations. If you can focus on your goal, and see how the other people are aiding you in having that, it can loosen up the tendency to harp on the things which you don't like. Maybe the second violinist has a habit of drooling, but so long as he is drooling on his own violin and not on yours, and can still play his part pretty well...

## Chamber Music Coaches

For chamber music, having a good coach can be a big asset. It can help neutralize the jockeying for control between players, as well as helping the group improve musically.

## Influencing Groups in a Good Way

The last story in this book describes an inspiring way to influence the groups you participate in.

◆◆◆◆◆◆◆◆◆◆◆◆◆◆◆◆◆◆◆◆◆◆◆◆◆◆◆◆◆◆◆◆◆

# Finding Our Tribes

## Story: At Last I Have Friends

A woman once told me that throughout her life she had trouble making friends. All through school and into graduate school, where she studied microbiology, Karen just never seemed to be able to find satisfying friendships. It was lonely.

In her thirties Karen got interested in the hammer dulcimer. She enjoyed it immensely and spent many hours practicing. She also began attending music festivals where people played that type of music.

An interesting thing happened.

At these gatherings, she kept finding people that she really enjoyed being with. Soon she had many rich relationships, and had developed a group of close friends. She was impressed with how easy and natural it was for her.

She told me, with mystified awe in her voice, that a number of times while at the music festivals, she found herself looking up at a new person she did not know, and there would be an instant connection. From that point forward, they were friends. It was immediate.

This was nothing like her struggles in the past – trying to build a friendship over time and never really quite feeling connected.

When we are being totally authentic and living in the easy flow of who we really are, it is easy to connect with other people who are "on our wavelength," and who feel like part of "our tribe."

A trap that many of us fall into is *trying to be different than we are so that people will like us better*. People may respond to us better if we act the way they want us to, but if we do that, the quality of our connection with them is not going to be deeply satisfying.

It takes effort to play roles that are not authentic. Keeping up the charade drains a lot of life-force energy. There is also the worry that if the other person finds out who we *really* are, they will be angry or abandon us. The whole thing can be exhausting, nerve-wracking and disheartening. It certainly is a surefire way to steal both our joy in life and the pleasure in our relationships.

Spending time doing the things we enjoy most is a good way to find that track where we are naturally in the flow of our well-being. Being in that state is like a magnet that draws in other people who will truly appreciate us.

*Our tribes are waiting for us.*
*To find them,*
*do what resonates with your soul's desire.*

◆◆◆◆◆◆◆◆◆◆◆◆◆◆◆◆◆◆◆◆◆◆◆◆◆◆◆◆◆◆◆◆◆◆

CHAPTER SEVENTEEN

# Performing At Your Best

This chapter includes:

## 1. INTERNALIZING YOUR PIECE

## 2. WAYS TO SOLIDIFY A PIECE
- Different Tempos
- Distractions
- Give It Time to Digest
- Make a Recording – Sound, Video
- Playing In Front of a Practice Audience

## 3. DEALING WITH STAGE FRIGHT
- Overall Approach
- Handling the Extra Energy
- Know That Fear Does Not Need To Stop You
- Avoid Stimulants

## 4. PERFORMING IS A PACKAGE
It's Not Just Playing the Music

## 5. AUDITIONING

## 6. CONCERTS & RECITALS

There is always more we could do to improve our overall technique, but having an upcoming performance is an opportunity to set clear goals, and finish something with a feeling of accomplishment and closure.

Knowing the performance date gives us a timeframe. It helps us pace how we work on a piece, organize our practice time and, if necessary, it can inspire us to give it an extra push when the time is getting close.

The pieces we chose to perform also divide our music studies into sections, and can inspire us to develop the techniques which are needed to perform particular pieces.

## 1. INTERNALIZING YOUR PIECE

Just knowing how to play a piece is not good enough for performing. The best is to internalize the piece to the extent that we could play it even if we were not thinking about it.

### Skating on Thin Ice
When I was a kid, we looked forward to freezing weather because it meant the ponds would freeze, and we could go skating. But we couldn't skate until the ice was thick enough. If ice is 2" thick or 12" thick, it looks smooth on the surface, but if you put weight on thin ice it breaks; thick ice will hold weight.

This is a good metaphor for performing a piece of music. We first get to a point where we can play the piece (the pond looks smooth and frozen), but then **we need to solidify the piece** (we need to be able to play it under pressure).

Unexpected things can come up in a performance, and we need to be able to continue despite the challenges.

### What kinds of challenges?

- Something distracts me; I lose concentration for a moment.
- I feel intimidated or get nervous when I perform.
- I am in a different environment – in my teacher's studio or on a concert stage, instead of at home where I practice.
- My health is not good – I could have a cold, a fever, a broken leg, a sore back, aches or pains.
- I have had an emotional shock – someone died, a relationship ended, I had an argument, someone insulted me or said something hurtful to me.
- I feel uncomfortable or strange wearing my concert clothes.

Any of the above challenges will test the solidity of the piece. They could *crack the ice* if it is not thick enough. If the ice is thick, I will still be able to function and play the piece well. If it is not, things are likely to go wrong.

### "I Played it Better At Home"

Every violin teacher has heard (hundreds of times for many of us) a bewildered student say in a lesson, "But I played it better at home." One teacher I know even has a plaque saying that in her studio.

What these students don't understand yet is that being able to play a piece under ideal conditions without any stressful factors is great, but it's just a start. There is now a smooth surface of ice on the pond, but if it cracks under pressure, it is not thick enough yet. It is time to solidify that piece!

## 2. WAYS TO SOLIDIFY A PIECE

- DIFFERENT TEMPOS
- DISTRACTIONS
- GIVE IT TIME TO DIGEST
- MAKE A RECORDING – Sound, Video
- PLAYING IN FRONT OF A PRACTICE AUDIENCE

**DIFFERENT TEMPOS**
Your piece will be much more solid if you are not restricted to just one tempo. You should be able to play it well at both a faster and slower speed. Use the metronome for this.

***Remaining At Ease***
When you play your piece in the faster tempos, you are not trying to give yourself the feeling of playing FAST, you are playing it at a faster tempo and continuing to feel comfortable and in control of things. It is never a good idea to practice feeling rushed or out of control.

Likewise, you should have the presence and control to be able to slow it down. Don't let your body dictate the speed of the piece for you (like playing faster to avoid running out of bow). Be sure you can maintain control at a slower tempo.

**DISTRACTIONS**
***While still playing with ease and accuracy***

If you can play a piece with all sorts of additional challenges, that will make it more solid. For each of the following suggestions, your goal is to be able to play the piece in an easy and accurate way.

## *Types of Challenges:*

- Body Position
- Bow Hold
- Distracting Sounds
- Walk, Dance, Move Your Body
- Clothing
- Different Locations

Play in an easy tempo. You will probably need to use the metronome to "keep you honest" with the tempo. It is easy to start speeding up when we know something very well.

If you make mistakes, play it again without the distraction. Then try it *with* the distraction again. Keep working on it until you can play it with the distraction and still play with ease and without mistakes.

## Body position
Play the piece with your body in different positions.

*Examples:*
- Standing with one foot on a chair
- Sitting on the floor
- Lying on the floor
- Balancing on one foot
- Sitting on something low or high
- Sitting with your feet up
- Leaning against something

### Bow Hold

Hold the bow in a different way. *Examples*:

- Reverse the bow and hold it near the tip
- Hold the bow in your fist
- Hold the bow further up the stick nearer the balance point
- Use only the middle two fingers and thumb on the bow
- Put your thumb on the underside of the frog, instead of on the stick

### Distracting Sounds

People in your family can have fun with this one. They can:

- Clap at an unexpected moment
- Start telling the player a story
- Laugh or sing
- Turn on the radio and sing along loudly, dance and clap
- Make weird sounds, then laugh hysterically

If you don't have anyone to distract you, you can:

- Put on some other music that will distract you
- Watch a television show or movie while playing

### Walk, Dance, Move Your Body

Think of marching bands or Irish step dancers. See if you can devise your own movements to do while you play.

- March to the music
- If your piece is in 3, do a waltz as you play
- Imagine you are a gypsy violinist strolling at a restaurant and seducing the restaurant patrons with your charms

**Clothing**

Be sure to play your music a number of times wearing the shoes and clothing that you intend to wear in an upcoming performance.

*Suggestions*:

• Heavy winter boots

• Sunglasses (this is a very good one)

• Outdoor jacket

• Baseball cap

• Wide-brimmed hat (this is especially good because it will change the way your instrument sounds to you)

• Winter ski cap

• Wearing a scarf or shawl

• Your concert clothes and shoes!

## Getting Comfortable in Your Concert Clothes and Shoes

If you are planning to wear high heels, it is good to wear those while practicing you recital pieces. Your posture will be different than in your bare feet or running shoes.

As you play, move your weight from foot to foot to keep your posture flexible and free.

One young man used to ride the subway in his tux so that he would feel more comfortable wearing it during concerts.

## Different Locations

Part of what can be intimidating about performing is being up on a stage with bright lights shining at you. Being able to play your piece in odd places can help with this. *Suggestions*:

- Play in every room of the house
- Play outdoors
- Play in the garage
- Stand on the stairs or the landing between stairs
- Stand on a coffee table or bench
- Stand in the bathtub
- Watch yourself play in the bathroom mirror
- Position some lights so they are shining in your eyes
- Play in an empty recital hall or other place where concerts are held or the largest space you have access to
- Turn off some lights, so it is difficult to read the music

### Coming Up With Creative Distractions Can Be Lots of Fun

Many kids who come for lessons with their parents or other siblings have fun with the distractions. Younger siblings enjoy coming up with new challenges for their older brother or sister, and it is a great feeling for the player to be able to triumph over a new challenge. "I can even play it lying down!"

To add a bit more suspense to the game, the ideas can be put on slips of paper and pulled out of a jar.

Below is a story that shows the importance of being able to play under many different conditions.

### Story: Iiiiiiizzzzzzzzzz-zzzzz-zzzz!

For a number of years I played in a trio that provided classical music for formal parties and weddings. We were pleased to be hired for a job playing at the elegant Rosecliff Mansion in Newport, RI. The bride was an anchor woman for a television news show, so there were people with large television cameras recording the whole event. Along with the cameras came an elaborate array of stage lights that were carried on poles out to the back lawn where the wedding ceremony took place.

They could not have asked for a more picturesque setting with the wide lawn edged by rocky cliffs and the open ocean beyond. Behind us was the imposing mansion with its manicured gardens. The tasteful wedding decorations augmented its already regal elegance on this special day.

Or special *evening*, as this, being a Jewish wedding ceremony, was scheduled to begin just after sunset.

As the sun was setting, we played trios by Mozart and Haydn while the guests assembled. When we got the signal, we started the processional. There were a number of people in the wedding party – children, bridesmaids and groomsmen, two sets of grandparents, the groom and his parents and finally the bride with her parents.

Each set of people began at the mansion, processed down the terrace steps, walked across a flat area, then up another set of steps, a short walk and then down more steps to the lawn. Then there was quite a distance across the lawn to where we all were waiting. Giving each set of people their time in the spotlight, the next set would wait inside the mansion until the previous set had processed all the way to the front.

The grandparents were not as spry as they probably once were. And our processional music became an endless loop as we repeated the various sections over and over. In 20 years of playing weddings this was the longest processional by far!

Meanwhile, dusk had set in and our stage lighting sent out an all-points alert to every mosquito within a 2-3 mile radius. "Come to the wedding, bare flesh available and people unable to slap."

The mosquitos were biting my arms, neck, face, ankles, hands, fingers... the fingers were the worst part. I now had the music memorized, so could watch as the mosquitos landed on my fingers and filled up on my blood. I felt like my whole body was a mass of bites, and there was nothing I could do to stop them.

Not to complain because the flutist had it worse. They landed on her lip while she was playing and bit her there. When she inhaled quickly to grab a breath between phrases, a mosquito met its end as it went into her mouth.

Finally, finally, the bride and her parents arrived – at long last! I was able to cover as much of my body as possible while we waited it out through the ceremony. Meanwhile the stage lighting had shifted away from us and was centered on those in the front.

The young starlets (the bridesmaids) sat in front of the television cameras with their classic black velvet dresses – bare shoulders and arms with much of their backs exposed as well.

I marveled at their self-controlled poise in front of the cameras as I (no longer in the spotlight) swatted mosquitos as discreetly as possible.

There was one more challenge when at last the recessional came. As the wedding party left, the stage lighting which had provided lighting for the whole affair, left along with them. We finished our work that evening playing from memory in the dark.

Later during the cocktail hour, there was some comic relief as a guest related to us in an unfettered Texan drawl that he had watched as a mosquito landed on the back of one of the blond starlets in the bare-shouldered dresses in front of him. "I was watching as it landed on her and just sucked that blood right up. I didn't know whether to slap her or *what!*"

**Moral of the story:** A professional needs to be able to perform even when the conditions are not ideal.

## GIVE IT TIME TO DIGEST

Memories are stored in different ways in our brains. Short term memory is different from long term memory.

Good cooks know that certain foods taste better if the flavors have a chance to blend. When they marinate meat, they allow time for the flavors to really absorb. Likewise, we also play best when a piece has had time to "marinate" and sink in a bit.

What I have found during my years of teaching is that people usually need to be able to play their piece well at least one month before the recital. During that last month, they can solidify it with the techniques described above. If they can't play their piece well a month in advance, there could be some unhappy moments at the recital.

## MAKE A RECORDING – SOUND, VIDEO

We are lucky to have so many recording options now – cell phones that shoot video and also have a recording apps, digital recorders, cameras with video functions, camcorders, laptop web cameras. You probably have at least one of these. Use it to help you prepare for your recital or concert.

If you make a video of yourself playing your piece each day, you will be able to fix many things on your own, even without the help of your teacher.

If you get a good video or recording, you can keep it in an archive of your performances, too!

## PLAYING IN FRONT OF A PRACTICE AUDIENCE

### *Practice audiences*
- Play for each member of your household
- Play for neighbors or friends
- Play for coworkers or at your parents' workplace
- Play for Grandma over the telephone.
- Stuffed animals make a friendly audience

## 3. DEALING WITH STAGE FRIGHT

- OVERALL APPROACH
- HANDLING THE EXTRA ENERGY
- KNOW THAT FEAR DOES NOT NEED TO STOP YOU
- AVOID STIMULANTS

Many of us have a certain amount of nervousness about performing. For some, it is so intense that one could call it stage fright. Here are some suggestions.

## OVERALL APPROACH

### *Be prepared. Know your piece well.*

Knowing that you are not really well prepared can add a lot of fuel to a bit of nervousness. Give yourself the gift of having "done your homework." At least you will know that you have internalized your piece to the extent that you will be able to play it whether you are nervous or not. The techniques outlined above (distractions, etc.) are good ways to help you achieve that end.

### *The audience wants you to do well, too.*

In our minds, *The Audience* can become this group of critical people. In reality this is not so. **The people in the audience want to have a pleasant experience.** Watching someone feel devastated, is not what they signed up for. They want to see and hear you do well. They *want* you to do your best, just the same way that you do. They are your friends and allies.

Even a music critic would rather hear an inspired performance than have to sit through someone not doing well.

*Only compare yourself to your own best self.*
You are not going out on stage to be Itzhak Perlman. Your job is to be *you*. The person to measure yourself against is your-own-self-functioning-at-your-full-potential.

## Story: The Winning Basketball Coach

A winning basketball coach was asked about how he was able to switch teams and still have the team he was coaching win the championship.

His secret? For each player there were particular skills he was helping them improve. He worked with the players individually, always encouraging and pushing them to better their own skills and contributions to the team.

He never compared them to the competition and never even talked about winning a game! What he was striving for was that the players each play at their greatest potential. That is where he put the focus. And he got results!

## HANDLING THE EXTRA ENERGY

Until we try it, we don't know how our body chemistry will react to performing. For most people there will be more energy that starts flowing, but the only way to find out is to do it.

### Do a lot of performing

Part of what can make performing difficult is that a person can experience something like a mild form of shock. It's a brand new experience; he doesn't know what will happen. His animal self is put on high alert, *fight or flight*.

But if we perform repeatedly, the newness and shock wear off. We cannot stay on such high alert for very long. In the same way that playing a particular passage 100 times gives us greater ease with it, the more we perform, **the more we can anticipate the experiences and the results our body's inner pharmacy may bring about.**

So the good news is that the more we perform, the better we get at knowing how to focus and handle our energy when we are on stage. A good way to approach this is to move into it a bit at a time. My students prepare for our recitals by playing repeatedly in front of progressively larger audiences. First they play for me as the teacher, then for their families, a stranger, more people, the dress rehearsal, and finally the recital.

If you don't do any of the preparatory performances, you really are not giving yourself a good chance at doing your best when the big day arrives. **Not only do we need to practice our piece, but also to practice performing, if we are to be well prepared.**

### *Playing too fast*

It is common that when our hearts start to beat faster and the adrenaline starts to flow, we start to play faster. But this can lead to what musicians call a *train wreck*.

After a few train wrecks people learn that their *impression* of the speed can get distorted if they get nervous. To control it they learn to **play at a speed that feels slow to them but is probably the same speed they normally play the piece.**

## KNOW THAT FEAR DOES NOT NEED TO STOP YOU

Knowing through our own personal experience that fear does not need to stop us from doing what we want to do is one of the great gifts of learning to play the violin.

This is an exceedingly valuable thing to know.

### Story: *Playing Through Her Fear*

Lisa took violin lessons with me from the time she was in 6th grade until she graduated from high school. When she started, she was moving into that age when most people feel pretty insecure. For a young teenager to get up in front of an audience and do something brand new that she wasn't very good at yet was a real challenge. Helping Lisa to be able to perform with confidence was going to be an important part of our lessons.

Lisa was smart and had a terrific personality. She was not rebellious or contrary, but listened well and did her best to follow my directions and suggestions.

I really wanted her to have a good experience with performing, so I did my best to set things up so that we would have the greatest chance at success.

For her first recital, we chose a piece that would be very easy for her. I also suggested that I play along with her in the performance. That way she would not be alone on the stage, would not need to be stressed about the difficulty of the notes, and if she missed something I would keep playing and she could just get back in.

We worked on solidifying her piece, and I told her repeatedly that our goal was that we go out on the stage and play through the piece. It was not important if she made mistakes. If she just was able to get through it, that would be enough to call it a success.

**First recital:** Lisa did it. She played her piece, even though she was visibly shaking all over. There were mistakes, but SHE DID IT. She did not let fear stop her.

**Next recital:** It was a bit better. She was still nervous, made some minor mistakes, but GOT THROUGH IT AGAIN and was not shaking so visibly anymore.

**Next recital:** Even better. And on it went through the years.

When Lisa turned 16 she was nervous about taking her drivers' test, but we talked about it, and I reminded her that she had now learned to do something even if she was feeling fear.

She passed her drivers' test the first time.

When Lisa graduated from high school she was the valedictorian of her class. To this day, on the wall in the studio, I have a newspaper clipping of her wearing her graduation cap and gown, standing at the podium and addressing the whole town on behalf of her class. Bravo!

---

This is one example of how studying music can teach us skills that will come to our aid again and again as we navigate through the challenges, triumphs, twists and turns of our lives.

## AVOID STIMULANTS

### *Story: A French Menu*

I was playing in an orchestra on a concert tour in France. We had rehearsed the music for this tour extensively so I felt very confident of it. I was not a principal player, so there wasn't any particular personal pressure on me. In each city we played the same program, so it was definitely a low-stress type of performing.

Before one of the concerts, some of my colleagues and I had a meal at a local restaurant. The only options were three different set menus. These included a number of courses, followed by dessert and coffee.

Not having been a coffee drinker for years, I would not have ordered coffee after my meal, but since it was included and smelled so good, I drank it. That evening I was a nervous wreck during the whole concert. I knew that there was no reason to be nervous, but my body had other ideas.

I learned my lesson with that experience. Thank goodness I was not playing a solo.

You may not be affected by coffee or other stimulants in this way, but let this story be a heads up to be extra aware about what you eat or drink before a concert or recital.

## 4. PERFORMING IS A PACKAGE
### *It is Not Just Playing The Music*

A common mistake is for a person to only practice the actual piece of music that he will perform, forgetting that the performance is a total package. Pity if he walks out awkwardly, doesn't know how to bow (more awkwardness), gets flustered putting his music out, isn't clear about how to start the piece... It can begin to look like a comedy routine. The audience doesn't want to be empathizing with all a performer's awkwardness.

All those little things (bowing to the audience, etc.) are so much easier to learn than playing the violin. Don't let them detract from all that you have worked so hard to achieve. When you are comfortable and confident the audience will be more relaxed, too, and they will enjoy it more.

---

**BOWING Before and After Your Performance**

1. Bring your feet together first. Bowing with your feet spread apart looks pretty amusing.
2. Let the tip of your bow point downward or up in the air, not at the audience.
3. It is nice to smile at the audience just before you bow.
4. Lean over, look down at your shoes, and count to ten.

You are doing the audience a favor by just bowing in a normal natural way. A strange or awkward bow may make more of an impression than the music itself.

---

Take some time to feel secure with all the elements that go along with performing your piece.

### *Elements to include in your performances:*

1. Before walking out on stage affirm to yourself what you goal is.

2. Walk out.

3. It is nice to smile at someone you like in the audience.

4. Bow towards the audience, look down and count 1-10 (see text box on page 209).

5. Put your music on the stand, if you are using music. Note that this is *after* the bow.

6. Think of how your piece will sound, so you know what you are doing before you start.

7. PLAY.

8. Often it is good to freeze for just a moment when you finish playing. Imagine there are extra beats at the end of the piece.

9. Feet together.

10. Bow (see text box about bowing, page 209).

11. Acknowledge your accompanist, if you did not bow together.

12. Collect your music.

13. Walk off.

14. Congratulate yourself. This is a way to create a positive imprint in your subconscious about performing.

**All of these elements are part of your performance.**

## 5. AUDITIONING

Unlike a concert or recital, an audition is a test. You will pass or fail and often be given a numerical rank. In this case they will deduct points for any deviation from what it says in the rules.

### Follow the Rules

Of course you want to play all the correct rhythms and notes with good intonation, the correct dynamics, good phrasing and good tone. But for an audition the focus also needs to be on following directions. What is it they are looking for?

If it is a high school all-state audition and they want 3-octave scales in a particular rhythm at a particular metronome speed, do it just the way they have specified.

Get the correct edition of the auditioning piece and follow the fingerings and bowings in that edition. Photocopies are only acceptable to avoid page turns.

Listen to recordings and find out what the accepted tempo for that piece is. Don't play it faster or slower.

### Your Goal Is Accuracy

Although they would like you to play musically and with expression, your primary focus should be ACCURACY.

### Be Respectful, Have A Likeable Personality

Another important aspect of auditioning well is to be respectful. Whether it is an all-state judge, a college end-of-semester jury, or an orchestral auditioning committee, these people are judges. They want to be treated with respect.

People are influenced by a person's physical appearance. If you show up for an all-state audition with ratty jeans, your friends may think you look cool, but the judge probably will not. The judge will take much more kindly to you if they feel you are taking this seriously and are cooperative and diligent.

## ORCHESTRA AUDITIONS

For orchestra playing the priorities are as follows:
#1 is Rhythm
#2 is Intonation (notes in tune)
#3 is Musicality, including playing in a way that is
  stylistically correct for each era
#4 is Tone (sound quality)

**Important:**
1. Be sure to make the rests the correct length.
2. Careful not to rush rapid passages of fast notes. That is a big no-no!
3. Many people auditioning spend more time preparing their solo piece than the orchestral excerpts. That is a big mistake. The auditioning committee wants to know what you will contribute to the *orchestra*.
4. The notes may be easier in Mozart, but that is also where your weaknesses can be most obvious, especially keeping a steady tempo. Prepare the Mozart excerpt extremely carefully, *with the metronome.*

The same applies for auditions for scholarships and the end-of-semester juries for music students. Project an image of someone who is serious about playing their game, as well as playing your instrument well. Students who come across as contrary, arrogant, self-absorbed or disrespectful in any way, are not winning any points here, and are losing them for sure.

Even if you will be playing an orchestral audition behind a screen, dress well. The orchestra manager, or whoever is working with the people who are auditioning, should also see you as a respectful team player.

## Story: His Personality Disqualified Him

A violinist once told me that she went to audition for an orchestra and was taken aback when she heard another violinist warming up in the room next door.

What she heard was an exquisite sound, flawless technique, playing at a standard much higher than her own. Should she just go home? She went ahead and did the audition, even though she didn't think she would get the job. She wasn't hired, but neither was the violinist next door. Why?

It turned out he came from the New York Philharmonic and had been fired because of his difficult personality. His reputation preceded him, and he could not even get a job in a part-time orchestra.

**Orchestras want team players**, not "bad apples that will ruin the bunch." If you are auditioning for an orchestra job, put yourself in the mindset of doing your part to benefit the group.

## 6. CONCERTS & RECITALS
### *Make It Your Gift to The Audience*

The people in the audience want to have a pleasant experience. They may be music lovers, people who care about you, or people who were obligated to attend for some reason. All of them are giving you some of their time.

Giving someone our time and focus is giving someone part of our lives. We each have a limited number of minutes within which to experience life. If someone gives you their time and focus, make it worthwhile for them.

Let your desire be to give those people listening something back. Play for *them*, not for yourself. All those many hours of practicing can be for you, but **when you walk out on the stage, play for the people who are listening.** It is not about you. It is about them. Be generous in your focus and desire.

Most people in the audience would much prefer to have an experience that touches them or lifts their spirits than hear someone play all the correct notes in a boring way. Make it as beautiful as you can, let the notes sing, put some heart and soul into it if you can.

Remember, they would much rather you create a wonderful experience for them, than watch you get all involved in your own self-judgment. This is not a test. It is a chance to give something of yourself to others.

◆◆◆◆◆◆◆◆◆◆◆◆◆◆◆◆◆◆◆◆◆◆◆◆◆◆◆◆◆◆◆◆◆

# In Life: Fear Does Not Need to Stop Us

# Handling Emotions

Emotions are powerful. They are the motivators for much of what we do, and they can push people to do things they normally would not think to do. There is a reason we have the term "crimes of passion."

There is a Buddhist practice where a monk will try to antagonize another monk. That way the one being antagonized can learn to handle the emotions that come up and have mastery over them. Many of us didn't get such good training. Our parents and the other adults in our lives were often not very good at handling their emotions. It can feel like the blind leading the blind as we bumble along doing our best in the situations we find ourselves.

Athletes, airline pilots, and people doing any kind of performing or competing, have to develop strategies that allow them to function well when the emotions are running high. **We each have our own personal pharmacy built into our bodies which produces our fluctuating body chemistry**. Adrenaline, oxytocin, dopamine, serotonin, testosterone, peptides, hormones... we swim in a sea of emotional reactions that can be stormy or calm. How well are we at navigating through those?

Here are some suggestions for working with fear/nervousness or other strong emotions when you are performing, playing or competing.

1. **Keep your sovereignty**; employ the power of your will and focus. This is your life. *You* are the one who determines this event's meaning and importance to you.

2. Let your focus be on **navigating to your goal** as you ride the energy that pours through.

3. **Don't pretend** an emotion does not exist, that you are not nervous, fearful, upset, etc. The emotions are part of the experience.

4. If possible, **channel the extra power** of the emotion in the direction that will serve you and help you achieve your goal. Many athletes and performers find that having that extra edge focuses their intent and enhances their power. One professional basketball player told me that he played best when he was angry.

**Rehearsing in *Small Time* to prepare for the *Big Time***
Just as we prepare for a violin performance by doing rehearsals and mini-performances, you can find ways to prepare for things in life by finding activities that are similar but on a smaller scale, and using them as practice for a bigger event.

*Knowing how to*
*ride the heightened energy of performing*
*is an art in itself.*

◆◆◆◆◆◆◆◆◆◆◆◆◆◆◆◆◆◆◆◆◆◆◆◆◆◆◆◆◆◆◆◆

# CHAPTER EIGHTEEN

# Reviewing and Looking Back

Going back to pieces we have played in the past can bring us benefits, satisfaction, and pleasure. Here are a few.

### 1. It's easier now!

It is gratifying to play a piece that was once a challenge and to see how much easier it is to play now. It is a nice way to see your improvement.

### 2. Upgrades are now possible.

You can build on what you have learned in the interim since you first played the piece, and take the piece to a new level. You can incorporate new skills and techniques. Maybe try some new fingerings or bowings.

### 3. Faster tempos

It may be easier to play it faster now, or to control a slower tempo. Check the old metronome markings and see how it feels now to play it at that speed. What speed would you choose now?

### 4. It gives you a dependable repertoire.

Reviewing past pieces keeps them under your fingers. You might be asked to play at church or suddenly need to play for a funeral; a friend might ask you to play; your parents might want to show you off for some visiting relatives; a scholarship opportunity or audition might come up. It is good to have a repertoire of music which you can play at any time should the need arise.

### 5. Better understanding of the musical ideas

The musical ideas may not be readily apparent to us when we first are getting acquainted with a piece. You may have just been happy to get the right notes, with the right rhythms, at a good tempo. Now the music itself can come through more, as well as how it fits into the style and era in which it was written.

### 6. Deeper layers revealed

Especially with phrasing, when we come back to a piece you may have a new sense of the phrases and the underlying structure and direction of them. The deeper layers and larger concepts become more apparent when we come back to it later.

### 7. The "flavor" gets enhanced.

The longer we know a piece of music, the more time it has to "age" in our memory. Like a good cheese or wine, it will take on a different flavor the longer it has been stored in your memory bank.

### 8. Like visiting an old friend

Going back to a piece we felt affection for can be like visiting an old friend. The warmth of remembrance can be a balm to the heart, or like the warm embrace of someone after a long, long time. And that friend may tell you new secrets.

## Story: *Playing the Same Pieces for 20 Years*

For more than 20 years, I played in a trio that played classical music for various formal parties, functions, weddings, etc. Our repertoire (mostly Mozart and Haydn) was the same for all those years, so we probably performed each of those pieces hundreds of times.

During that time, my relationship to those pieces went through different stages. What was at first interesting became boring over time. Later, that was replaced by a comfortable familiarity.

Every once in a while, it was as though a curtain would be lifted, and I would suddenly see a new layer to the music that had eluded me during the previous repetitions.

Sometimes there would be substitute players. Each one would have their own interpretation of what the composer was communicating, so that could bring a freshness and would sometimes give me new ideas about the pieces as well.

If I was not being paid to play those pieces so many times, I cannot imagine that I ever would have, but I received more than just the money earned. It gave me the opportunity to learn about the potential when one plays a piece so many times.

Like a vibrant marriage, where two people are continually learning and deepening their relationship, playing the same piece repeatedly over time can be surprising, expanding and enriching, as well as reassuringly comfortable.

◆◆◆◆◆◆◆◆◆◆◆◆◆◆◆◆◆◆◆◆◆◆◆◆◆◆◆◆◆◆◆◆◆◆◆◆◆◆

# The Value of Updating Our Relationships

When we have experiences, our versions of what took place often do not match with other people's versions of what happened. Even watching a movie, two people will remember different things about it and put their own interpretations on it.

### Story: The Look That Said It All

During the movie, the heroine had been through all sorts of dramatic turmoil. The climax in the final scene is a close up of the woman's face. That final moment held all that she had experienced throughout the film.

Instead of projecting any particular emotion, the director told her, "Think of nothing at all." What he wanted was a blank canvas. That way each person watching would project their own ideas and emotions onto what they thought she was feeling at that moment.

---

I notice how different each person's versions of things are when my Egypt travelers share their photos of a trip. One person's trip photos are full of people, and another person from the same tour does not have any people in his pictures at all. Another person looks up to photograph windows and arches above doorways, while someone else is photographing the cat sleeping in the same doorway.

## *Frozen in Time*

When we remember the situations we have experienced, it is our own personal version that comes up on the screen of our minds. What goes along with that is that the people and things in our memories become, in a sense, frozen in time. If we don't see someone again, we don't know who that person is *now*.

> We only have our own unique interpretation
> of who a person was at some point in the past.

Just as coming back to previous musical pieces gives us a chance to update our relationships to them, updating our versions of other people brings us closer to what is true in the present. This is especially helpful when we have had an unpleasant experience with someone, and they have changed for the better.

## *Story: THAT is Katie Now?*

I was happy to have a chance to update my idea about a violin student who took lessons at the school where I teach. I coached her in a high school string quartet as part of a summer program. She was a real asset to the group. She had a great attitude, learned her part and played it well, and encouraged the whole group with her "Let's go for it!" attitude.

My previous version of her had been in my head for years, and was constructed from the stories her first violin teacher had told me. Katie was a handful, to say the least. Even with her mother there at the lessons, she screamed and ran around, climbed under the piano, refused to play... she even scratched the dirt out of the plants in the studio. I was more than happy to replace that with the new version of Katie in my mind!

### *Updating relationships with your new skill levels*

When you come back to a piece of music you learned as a beginner, you can play it at a faster tempo because you are now more skilled. Likewise, when we develop our *Life Skills* we are better able to handle difficult situations and people that would have thrown us off course in the past.

If your Aunt Sally always used to get on your nerves, but now you can see her as she is, without feeling so enraged by her selfish behaviors, your new revised version of your relationship to Aunt Sally can be a welcome and empowering update.

Sometimes updating a relationship that has been difficult for us can have a profound impact.

### *Story: Just One Sentence...*

A friend of mine had been settled in a gay relationship for 18 years. Although Marvin's parents accepted his partner into their family, Marvin always knew his parents still wished he was not gay and was instead partnered with a woman.

When Marvin's father was close to death, Marvin and his mother spent a number of days sitting at his father's bedside. At one point Marvin's mother started in with, "What about that nice girl you used to like in high school..." It was painful for Marvin until all at once his father raised himself up and in a loud emphatic voice said, **"Sylvia, THE BOY IS OK."**

Marvin told me later that with that one sentence, years of pain, sorrow and despair were literally wiped out.

◆◆◆◆◆◆◆◆◆◆◆◆◆◆◆◆◆◆◆◆◆◆◆◆◆◆◆◆◆◆◆

# CHAPTER NINETEEN

# Using the Metronome

## Right on the beat!

We are lucky to have electronic metronomes today. A good loud steady click is a wonderful thing!

### The Taskmaster

Some people have a negative feeling about the metronome because they have had failures when using it in the past. They have the feeling that the metronome is telling them they are wrong, like a cold harsh judge who is reprimanding them.

If instead, they thought of the metronome as the bearer of good news, they would have a whole different feeling about it. If it brings success rather than failure, it becomes a valuable friend.

### It's dependable

If you think about it, playing with a metronome should be easier than playing with other people. At least it is absolutely steady and predictable. If I can't play with something that is completely dependable, that probably means that I am hoping everyone else will just keep adjusting to me, or maybe share my faults at exactly the same time?

### Story: Who is Right?

While I was in Germany, I played in a string quartet. In one of the pieces, the cellist kept rushing a particular passage. Different members of the group repeatedly tried to get him to slow down and keep the tempo steady. He kept insisting that he WAS keeping a steady tempo.

Finally, he was forced by the group to play the passage with a metronome. Of course it did not match up. "You see?!" said the first violinist triumphantly.

"No!" said the cellist. "The metronome is WRONG! It keeps changing!"

---

### So how can we be RIGHT with the metronome?

Here is one simple way. If you follow each step, it is a sure way to be able to have success with the metronome. If you are already pretty steady with the rhythms, you can leave some of the steps out.

## THE GOAL
To feel solid, sure and comfortable
while lining up with the metronome beats.

Playin' in the Groove.

*Strategy:*
## Synchronizing with the Metronome

### 1. Sing the passage with the metronome.

My students often laugh as I point to their heads and say the problem is not in their fingers or bow. If we are not really sure how it should sound, what are the chances of playing it the right way?

Using words for groups of rhythms can be helpful. You can make up your own. It can be fun to see what kids will come up with. It is best to use words that start with sharper sounds, like P, T, or K. Also, be sure that the emphasis is on the correct syllable in the word, so that it matches the rhythm you want.

*Examples*: Pepperoni-Pizza, Down-wiggle-Up-wiggle or Big-little-Big-little, Keep-it-even-Keep-it-even,... Different teachers each have the ones they like to use.

A handy way is if they all begin with P. The P goes with each metronome click. First, say only the P with each metronome click until it feels easy, then try Pepperoni (four 16ths), Pineapple (3 triplet 8ths) and Pizza (two 8ths) in different combinations. You can also do this while walking, instead of using the metronome.

### 2. Left hand fingers tap on your music.

Using one of your left hand fingers (violin fingering hand), tap on the music, touching each note in the rhythm of the piece with the metronome. Physically touching the notes with your fingers gives added benefits – kinesthetic and visual.

### 3. Tap a pencil on the stand with the bow hand.

Use you bow-arm hand with a pencil to tap on the stand. This will give a sharp, precise sound, which will either match the metronome beat or not.

### 4. Play it softly on the violin.

Now play it softly enough that you can still hear every beat of the metronome. Be careful that all the notes within each measure line up correctly, not just the down beats of the measures.

### 5. Play using the dynamics of the piece.

Play normally while still listening to hear the metronome beats.

### *Focusing Your Hearing*

See page 23 for a process using the metronome to develop your ability to focus your hearing for different distances: *Training Your Ability to FOCUS YOUR HEARING Away from the Sound of Your Instrument.*

### 6. Go back to Step #1 using a different tempo

---

## *The Note Values Are Rhythmic Proportions*

To really know the rhythms and have them internalized, you need to be able to keep everything in relationship in different tempos. The note values are really proportions, each relating to the other. **The more tempos you can correctly play your piece, the more the correct rhythmic proportions will become a part of you.**

## GOOD USES FOR THE METRONOME

- CREATING SUBDIVISIONS
  *Working Out Complex Rhythms*
- QUANTIFY IMPROVEMENTS
  *Setting A Goal Tempo*
- AND THE BEAT GOES ON!
  *Getting Through Without Stopping*
- NOTES IN OPPOSITION
  *Working Out Syncopations*
  *When First Learning To Do Syncopations*
  *Off Beats*

See also: pages 11, 32, 49, 62, 63-64, 67, 69, 82, 83, 112-114, 117, 130-131, 150, 161, 194. Also see the Index, page 257.
And STOP-PREPARE, *Getting It Right*, pages 6, 72-73, 96-97.

## CREATING SUBDIVISIONS

If you are playing a slow movement with long notes, you can put the metronome on a speed that will give you the subdivisions. This can be a great asset for projecting ornaments and faster note values that are interspersed with the long notes.

It will also prepare you to listen to another instrument that is playing faster notes during your long notes.

### Working Out Complex Rhythms

If your slow movement has $32^{nd}$ and $64^{th}$ notes that look complex and bewildering, you can change these to something which feels more familiar. Take the smallest note value and make that into one beat. Remember **rhythms really are just proportions**. You can change how they are written to make it easier to read while keeping the proportions the same.

*Strategy:*
## Using the Metronome on the Subdivisions

**1.** Put the metronome on 200. Make the 32$^{nd}$ notes get one beat, 16$^{th}$ notes get 2 beats, 8$^{th}$ notes get 4 beats, quarter notes get 8 beats (2 sets of 4), half notes get 16 beats (4 sets of 4).

**2.** Change the metronome to 100. Now there are two 32$^{nd}$ notes per beat, 16$^{th}$ notes get one beat, 8$^{th}$ notes get 2 beats, etc. You should still be playing exactly the same speed.

**3.** Move the metronome to 50. Now the 8$^{th}$ note gets one beat. You are still playing the same speed.

**4.** Go back to having the metronome on 100, and now move it up until you reach the tempo that suits the piece.

**5.** Keep alternating between having the click on the subdivisions and on the larger note values.

## QUANTIFY IMPROVEMENTS

Because the metronome is a numerical measure of speed, it can be a wonderful way to mark our improvements.

As we get more fluid with a set of actions we do often – for example, tying a shoe lace – we get faster at it without even trying.

Likewise, as we practice a piece of music it will get faster, even when we are not focusing on speed. People don't realize that it is faster, it just feels normal, unless they quantify it by checking what the metronome speed is.

Writing the metronome markings on your music and putting a date on them is a nice way to see your own improvement. This pleasure is even more enhanced when your goal is to play faster.

### Setting A Goal Tempo

You can have your teacher play the piece while you move the metronome to find the tempo that you would like to be able to play your piece. Write that metronome speed at the top of your music with the word, "Goal." Then write the tempo that you can now play it all the way through without making any mistakes. Put the date next to your present tempo.

> There is a lot of satisfaction to be had
> when you can see where you were
> and that
> you have now achieved what you wanted to.

## AND THE BEAT GOES ON!

One easy mistake to make when playing a piece is to hesitate, stop or repeat something that didn't work, rather than continuing to play. It's the "I'll just stop and fix that" or "I didn't get that right, I'll do it again." It is so natural to do this, but it can become a disability. The disability is that the person cannot play through the piece without stopping.

This is a tough one to fix once it has become entrenched. The metronome can be a big help with this. If you have a way of recording yourself, that can help, too.

See the story, **Breaking a Habit**, Chapter 7, page 88.

*Strategy (also described in Chapter 7):*
*Getting Through Without Stopping or Repeating*

**1.** Put the metronome on an easy tempo.

**2.** Resolve that you will keep going NO MATTER WHAT.

**3.** Turn on your recorder. This is a way to avoid fooling yourself (you could forget that you repeated something or hesitated). Making these mistakes becomes so second nature that people actually forget what they have done. The power of our mind to tell us *what we want to think* or not to remember is strong.

## NOTES IN OPPOSITION

### The pleasure of dissonance and opposition

Dissonance and opposition can be exciting and dramatic. Syncopations (playing opposite the beat), anticipations (a note that begins earlier than the harmonic structure supporting it) and suspensions (notes that hang on longer than the rest of the harmony) are the stuff of powerful music. They mirror our experiences in life, so they have vibrancy and appeal.

## WORKING OUT SYNCOPATIONS

The natural tendency with syncopations is to play them too early, with it getting worse the more syncopated notes you have in a row.

Here are two methods for getting the feel for doing them correctly. Once you have learned it, it will feel like a familiar dance step.

---

### FEELING THE MAIN BEATS,
even when you are only playing the syncopated notes,
### IS ESSENTIAL.

### *Strategy #1: Clapping*
Alternate clapping your hands with slapping your legs. The legs are the beats and the hands are the syncopations. Working with another person, one person does both hands and legs, and the other person does hands only (the syncopations). Keep switching who is doing the syncopations. Use the metronome to keep from speeding up.

### *Strategy #2: Metronome on the Subdivisions*
When you have syncopations in a piece, adjust the metronome to beat the subdivisions by doubling the metronome setting. Some metronomes also have the option of setting it to beat a 2, 3, or 4 rhythm. Rather than playing with a legato stroke, **play the syncopated notes with short bows that start with an accent, then fade out**, thus creating a pause during the main beats.

### *Moving your body on the beats*
It can also help to tap your foot or nod your head on the beats.

## WHEN FIRST LEARNING TO DO SYNCOPATIONS
### *Strategy: Double Bows*
First play **two bowed notes on each syncopated note** so that you have one bow stroke ON the beat and one stroke OFF the beat. First get the bows coordinated with the metronome, then start putting little **accents on the syncopated notes**.

## OFF BEATS, *pah-pah* and *chuck-chuck*

### *Um-pah-pah*

This rhythm is usually played DOWN-UP-UP. It is easy to rush the UP-UP (the off beats), so be careful. As a way to gain greater control, you can try this strategy:

1. Play any **one note repeatedly with all UP bows.** Have the metronome set on one click per UP bow. Play all the notes in the same place on the bow with a circular motion (not moving lower in the bow with each stroke). Find the easy, graceful motion that works. It is like a dance step with the bow.

2. **Play the passage with all UP bows**, both the *Ums* and the *pahs*, still using the circular strokes.

3. Play the passage **as written,** being careful that on the *pah-pah* UP bows you do not travel towards the frog but stay in the same location on the bow.

### *(Um)-chuck-chuck*

When the off-beat *chuck-chuck* is in the 2nd' violins and violas, DOWN-UP, and the *Um* is in the cello/bass.

With this rhythm, the natural tendency is to play early and lengthen the first *chuck* (the DOWN). Interestingly enough, this has become stylistic when playing Viennese waltzes, so no need to try to match the metronome on those. Play the DOWN early and too long, and the UP short.

◆◆◆◆◆◆◆◆◆◆◆◆◆◆◆◆◆◆◆◆◆◆◆◆◆◆◆◆◆◆◆◆◆

# The Pulse of Life:
## Living in Harmony or Dissonance

There is an ongoing flow and pulse in life that is beyond our control. When we are living in harmony with it, we have ease, contentment, and peace. When we are in dissonance with it, we do not.

If the inner response to something is, "No!" we are in opposition, and that brings about feelings of anger, sadness, grief, desperation, powerlessness and anxiety.

If it is something we have the power to change, this dissonance points out what to do. If the metronome is beating faster than it is possible to play with, we can move it down to a speed that is easier for us.

Likewise, in life, if something is within our control and we find ourselves upset by it, we can change it to better suit us. If I don't like the music playing on my car radio, I change it to another station or turn it off.

When I find myself in a situation where I am not in control, my only choice is to be in harmony with it or in dissonance, to move with it or to oppose it.

If I am playing in an orchestra and the tempo the conductor chooses is too fast for me, I cannot just slow it down (the way I could my metronome). I have to find a way to keep up. That could mean leaving out some of the notes, but if I try to play my own slower tempo I will lose my job in the orchestra.

## Hearing and Responding to the Pulse of Life

In order to play accurately with the metronome we need to:

• **Be able to hear it.**

• **Be willing to adhere to its pace.**

This is also true when living in sync with the great pulse of Life.

It may be beyond what most people think is possible or real, but the aim of the spiritual master is to listen deeply and profoundly to life's underlying pulse and flow. The masters know where to be at any given time, when to leave and when to arrive. That synchronizing of themselves with the greater *Pulse of Life* is their aim for each moment.

The captain of one the America's Cup Race sailboats was quoted as saying,

> *"Our aim is to discern the slightest change*
> *in the wind and respond to that immediately."*

This listening well and responding is not just good advice for winning a sailboat race, but for living a successful and effective life as well.

---

Those who listen and hear
the deep pulse and flow of life
know when to leave and when to arrive
in the right place at the right time.

---

CHAPTER TWENTY

# Entrainment and Sympathetic Vibration

## Baba Olatunji and Ray Charles

### Story: "Baba" Olatunji

During my years of playing in orchestras, I found it refreshing to also participate in the freedom and spontaneity of improvisation. One of my friends told me that the famous "Baba" Olatunji would be at an event in a nearby city. This was the man who introduced African drumming to North America in the 1950's. His *Drums of Passion* album (1959) sold over five million copies.

The hall was abuzz with excitement. There were lots of drummers, and African dancers, too. The drummers were from all over and many wanted to show off what they could do.

A lot of them were pretty self-absorbed and not listening to the group as a whole, but somehow the drumming began to organize. I soon figured out that Baba Olatunji was controlling the pace and overall direction of what was going on.

What a lesson for me to see the power and possibility of effective leadership! How was he able to do it?

He did not have a bigger, louder drum than anyone else, but **he had Presence; he was congruent**. Everything about him was unobstructed and consistent as he played his drum.

That powerful clarity and consistency had a much stronger influence on the group than the undisciplined showoffs. And soon the showoffs fell into the groove of the total group, and we all entered "The Zone."

---

## THE LAW OF ENTRAINMENT

The law of entrainment states that a group of vibrating bodies will eventually synchronize with the most powerful one. What is most powerful is not volume (loudness), but rather *consistency*.

It is natural for living things to be flexible and therefore to have inconsistencies. The one who vibrates in the most regular, consistent way will eventually dominate. Maybe not initially, but over time, those that are not as consistent will synchronize with the most consistent one.

### The power of a drone
(A drone is a continuous note which does not change)
When a group of singers does vocal improvisation in a room with florescent lights, they will eventually end up singing in harmony with the hum of the lights. That hum isn't very loud, but it is very consistent.

### Waltzing

If you have ever had the pleasure of waltzing with a good dancer, you will remember the joy of dancing with a grace you did not even know you had. Ahhh... It is no surprise that it is easy to fall in love with a man who can lead well on the dance floor.

### Devotees

Our tendency to entrain to a more congruent, and therefore more powerful, person is one reason why spiritual devotees want to be in the presence of spiritual teachers and masters. The devotees can more readily access their own spirituality as they entrain to a spiritual teacher's presence.

### More Examples of the Influence of Entrainment:

• In a chorus, when a weaker singer stands beside a stronger singer, the weaker singer will sing much better.
• A good bass drum player will coordinate a marching band.
• A student is influenced to play better when playing along with his teacher.
• Orchestral seating is usually with the stronger players in the front so that the rest of the section can more easily synchronize with them.
• One music teacher said he was able to coordinate his elementary school orchestra by plucking a bass line on an electric bass. It was much more effective than waving his arms!

## ENTRAINMENT THROUGH UNIFIED FOCUS

As well as synchronizing through sound, people can also unify through a shared focus, a shared breathing pattern, parallel body movements, and more. The more components combined, the more potent the synchronized event can become.

### Sporting events

One example of when this happens spontaneously is at big sporting events. If you have ever been outside Boston's Fenway Park during a baseball game and heard the crowd begin to cheer together... the power of it is amazing! I know there are many reasons for people to enjoy spectator sports, but one of the perks of being there in the stadium with all the other fans is the rush of the entrained group power when the crowd cheers together.

## Religions

When people sing hymns at church or chant at the ashram, they are synchronizing together through entrainment. They are focusing on the same thing by singing the words and melody together, and if they also breathe together at the end of each phrase, an even more powerful connection is created.

It is no surprise that groups which want their members to be unified, will have them sing, chant or do some sort of parallel motion together.

### Group Mind

Throughout time, armies have marched in rhythm together. That unified rhythm synchronizes them to form a *group mind* that can function as a well-oiled machine, and can also inspire the soldiers to perform heroic feats of service.

### Story: Ray Charles,
### An entrained group reacts together

During the years I worked as a freelance musician, I had the opportunity to play with a number of big name stars when they came to the area. The stars usually travel with a core of musicians to back them up. Local musicians are then hired to fill in on the other parts.

One evening I played in the backup orchestra for two concerts with Ray Charles. What a thrill! What an entrancing and charismatic musician he was. The audience was spellbound as they hung on each word he sang.

Because they were all so completely focused on him, and maybe even breathing along with the phrases of the songs, the audience entered into a group entrainment or *group mind*.

At the end of the concert, there was enthusiastic applause while Ray Charles bowed. Then he did a surprising thing. He went down on his knees in front of the audience in an ultimate act of humbleness.

The audience reacted as one person and immediately leaped to their feet, giving him a standing ovation while continuing to cheer. I had never seen anything quite like it. (Needless to say, I could not imagine an orchestra conductor doing that!)

Later that evening we played the second show. This time at the end when Ray Charles went down on his knees I was not so surprised, but the effect on the audience was identical.

As we say in the business, "He had them right in the palm of his hand."

### *Story: Germany before World War II*

When I was in Berlin, Germany, I saw a series of newsreels of Adolf Hitler addressing large crowds of people before WW II. At that time, Germany was in dire financial crisis. People felt vulnerable, unsteady, and worried about the future. Hitler was a commanding speaker, and I watched as the crowds attuned to him. The power in his voice sent out a vibration of solid strength, power and invincibility, along with an urgency to act.

The things that happened later could never have taken place if he had not been able to entrain the masses to his agendas. It was not his physical body nor his position in society that enabled him to garner the mass support, but the power of his voice certainly contributed by entraining people as they listened to him speak.

## SYMPATHETIC VIBRATION

For those of us who play stringed instruments, understanding sympathetic vibration is easier than it is for most other people. We can see and hear sympathetic vibration whenever we play a note (in tune) that resonates with one of the open strings.

The viola d'amore was designed to especially utilize these sympathetic vibrations by having another set of *sympathetic strings* underneath the strings which are played. These sympathetic strings resonate with the bowed notes which are played on the strings above.

## THE LAW OF SYMPATHETIC VIBRATION

A vibrating body will enliven other bodies which are at rest, if those at rest have the same resonating frequencies. The most noticeable sympathetic vibration is when both have the same fundamental. However, there will also be a response, if any of the notes in the harmonic series of that fundamental are sounded.

In other words, if I play the note A on the D string which matches the open A string note (a unison), the A string will begin to vibrate all by itself, without me touching it.

If I play the note A on the G string (one octave lower than the A string), the A string will also vibrate, because that A is the 1st harmonic of the fundamental note I am playing (the low A).

If I play an open D string, the A string will react just a bit, but not as much. The A which is an octave higher than the open string, is the 2nd harmonic for the fundamental note of D. So there is a relationship there, but not as strong as the other examples.

Every object and chamber has a fundamental resonating frequency. When this note is matched exactly, the sympathetic vibrations can become so intense that the form will shatter. This is the cause of the glass shattering when the soprano hits just the right note.

The concepts of entrainment and sympathetic vibration are now beginning to be applied in medicine, as well as a number of other fields.

◆◆◆◆◆◆◆◆◆◆◆◆◆◆◆◆◆◆◆◆◆◆◆◆◆◆◆◆◆◆◆◆◆◆◆◆◆◆◆◆◆

# One Person
# Can Make a Big Difference

## Itzhak Perlman

### SYMPATHETIC VIBRATIONS IN OUR LIVES

What we can see and hear happening with the strings on the violin, is also happening within us each day. We are resonating with people and things in our environment that match something within ourselves – feelings, ideas, desires, likes, dislikes, fears, hopes... Whenever there is something that finds a similarity within us, it is as though those strings within us begin to resonate.

One of the most popular songs ever written was "Yesterday" by Paul McCartney. Who has not experienced the disappointment and shock of a sudden heartbreaking change? "Yesterday, all my troubles seemed so far away..."

Now if that same melody had lyrics about excavating fossils in the desert, the broad appeal would not be there. The sympathetic vibrations of sameness would not vibrate in so many people.

## ENTRAINMENT and
## SYMPATHETIC VIBRATION COMBINED

As one might imagine, a combination of these two powerful responses (entrainment and sympathetic vibration) is even more potent. Think of the power of the almost 3,161,600 (in 2012) Muslims who came together to do the prayers – both the sound and movements – during the annual Hajj pilgrimage in Mecca. The attunement with a group of that size, with all those bodies, minds and emotions synchronized together, is a powerful experience for those who participate.

Once we become aware of the principles of entrainment and sympathetic resonance, we can begin to evaluate how we want to use them in our lives. We can also be more alert to how **influences may be augmenting things within ourselves that we do, and do not, want to feed and amplify.**

### Story: The" Observer" Journalist
I was interested to hear about a woman journalist who wanted to write a story about the drumming rituals of a tribe in Africa. Somehow she thought she could just go and observe without being involved in it herself.

What she had not factored in was that she would be like a fish in a fish tank with no way out or anywhere else to go. The drumming permeated every cell of her body. No amount of planning to "only watch," could change that.

Suddenly she found herself in the middle of it all, dancing wildly. So much for thinking she would "just watch!"

So it behooves us to **choose consciously** about what we will be surrounded by. Maybe better not to go to an African drumming unless you intend to dance or drum!

---

**If people have shared traits, those common traits increase in intensity when they are together.**

What this means is that if two people with shared traits are together, and one of them starts doing something, the second one will start doing it, too. When the second one parallels the first one's actions, words, thoughts, or emotions, **those will then be amplified in *both* of them.**

*Example*:
If I have strong political opinions and get together with someone else who focuses a lot on politics, we will both become more and more animated and opinionated.

*Example*:
If there is an angry person in a group, we may find ourselves getting angry, too. And if we don't want to get angry, then we may be irritated at that person (translate: angry) for being angry. Either way, we have begun to resonate with anger.

Excitement, hatred, fear and elation (like the home run at the ball game) are easy emotions to have amplified by others, especially in crowds.

## A QUICK REVIEW:

1. Groups will entrain to the person who has the most consistency. A person who has a steadfast, solid presence and who exhibits congruency can draw the others in a group into his or her way of acting or being.

2. If people have shared traits, the things that they have in common increase in intensity when they are together.

---

## How Can All This Be Used in a Beneficial Way?

Here is a story which I hope will inspire you. It feels like a good way to bring this book to a close.

## Story: A Concert with Itzhak Perlman

I had been playing with the orchestra for a number of years. During that time there were people who came and went, but most of the non-string players were consistent. There might be twenty violinists needed, but not many English horn players or harpists, so once the people playing those instruments had a job, they tended to hold onto it.

Orchestra members spend many hours working together in the shared quest of good musical performances. It is not unlike a big family, with the same sorts of feelings of companionship and camaraderie, as well as the difficulties that go along with that.

Musicians often have a strong memory for sound, and so it was through hearing each person play their instrument that we knew each other best. We might not even remember a player's name, but we certainly knew what to expect when it was their turn to play a prominent solo line.

Each concert usually had a concerto, and during the seventeen years I played with the orchestra, we had a number of marvelous musicians join us on the stage.

In October 1989 we were pleased to have Itzhak Perlman come to play the Tchaikovsky Violin Concerto. I had seen him perform a number of times, but this was the first time I was performing with him on the stage.

Unlike some of the other soloists, Itzhak Perlman was not *high maintenance*. There was no scuttlebutt about his needing special care or wanting us to rearrange things to better suit him. His attitude was relaxed, cheerful, and easy to work with.

That evening when he came out to play the concerto I was so impressed by what happened.

**Everyone in the orchestra played better!**

It was really quite amazing. All these people whose playing I was so familiar with, seemed to somehow have reached a new level in their playing. Everyone sounded better and afterwards seemed very pleased with his or her own personal performance, as well as the performance as a whole.

What happened?

During that time, I had become interested in hands-on healing and what is called *energy work*. As I was teaching others to work with the healing energy by feeling it in their hands, I started to be able to see it, too (not just feel it).

As we were playing the violin concerto, I switched into a broader-vision mode, to see if I could see what was going on with Itzhak Perlman.

Our *energy fields* are the areas around us that still contain some of who we are, even though it is outside our bodies. You may have been aware of this when someone got too close. They were "in your space." Or you may have felt the presence of someone behind you, even if you could not hear them.

Normally, I would see that a person's energy field was a short distance around them. It tends to get bigger when we are feeling expanded or expressive, and to get smaller when we are low energy or contracted.

With Itzhak Perlman what I saw was that his energy field was HUGE. It filled the entire concert hall! And the feeling of being in that field was so positive and good.

**It exuded generosity of spirit,**

**an appreciation of life**
**and**
**tremendous competence.**

Like the journalist who found herself saturated in the African drumming, we all – everyone in the orchestra, and I presume the audience, too – were saturated in this wonderful, positive space of generosity, appreciation, and in the case of the musicians, **competence.** What could be better to bring about a marvelous performance?

This influence happened through both sympathetic resonance and entrainment.

**The sympathetic resonance** happened as the *string* of competent musicianship within each of us, vibrated along with the competent musicianship Itzhak Perlman was expressing. That amplified the musicianship in each member of the orchestra.

**The entrainment** happened in a number of ways. First, we were all playing the same music together, and he was the soloist, so of course we were all tuned in to him. But we played concertos with wonderful musicians in every concert, so that aspect was not out of the ordinary.

However, this concert was extraordinary, in that we played so much better than we usually did.

So what was it?

I think the difference was the magnificence, size and congruency of his energy field. It had consistency (it did not have anything within it that was interfering with the flow). It saturated each one of us in his generous, competent, and unobstructed spirit.

We were all within it and filled by it. And just as the journalist found herself drawn in and dancing wildly to the drumming, we were drawn in and lifted to new heights of musicianship.

But, unlike the journalist who was alone while the drummers were many, this time it was **the many who were influenced by the one**.

What I learned from this was:

**One person can make a big difference.**

If we ever feel sorry about the state the world, our communities or our families, there IS something we can do. We can become a person who is so congruent and consistent within ourselves, that the best qualities of who we are can permeate every situation that we find ourselves in.

**And that's enough to keep anyone busy for a lifetime.**

◆◆◆◆◆◆◆◆◆◆◆◆◆◆◆◆◆◆◆◆◆◆◆◆◆◆◆◆◆◆◆◆◆◆◆◆

*Thank you.*

**Ruth E. Shilling**, M.M. (Viola Performance), has been teaching violin, viola, and chamber music to adults and children at the University of Connecticut CSA for more than 30 years. She piloted the *Violin for Adults* program for adult beginners, which has matured into an active chamber music program.

Ruth spent five years studying in Germany with Eberhard Klemmstein, previously of the Reger String Quartet and now the Director of the Erlanger Musikinstitut. During her time in Germany, Ruth played with the RIAS (Radio in the American Sector) Jugend Orchester, The Berliner Bach Gesellschaft, and the Berliner Barock Orchester; and made recordings with both RIAS and the Winsbacher Knabenchor.

In the USA Ruth was the principal violist of New London, Connecticut's Eastern Connecticut Symphony Orchestra, performing and recording with them for 17 years. During that time, she was also a member of the Hop River Chamber group, the Trillium Trio and the Minoan Quartet.

Ruth Shilling and her Students

Additional recordings made in the USA include the following albums:

*So Strong* with Justina & Joyce

*Awake, Arise, Ascend* with Connie Stardancer

*Keeper of the Holy Grail* with Richard Shulman

Ruth resigned from the ECSO after creating the *All One World Egypt Tours* business which has now taken her to Egypt more than 50 times.

◆◆◆◆◆◆◆◆◆◆◆◆◆◆◆◆◆◆◆◆◆◆◆◆◆◆◆◆◆◆◆◆◆◆◆

*Find SUCCESS with the Violin & Life online:*

• successviolin.com

• Facebook.com/successviolin* and Facebook.com/ruthshillingmm*
  * These pages can also be viewed by those who are not members.

• This book is available from Amazon.com and other bookstores.

• Other offerings from All One World: all1world.com.

Also by Ruth Shilling:

• **Playing the Violin & Viola with Vibrato** (ebook).

• **TONE: Violin & Viola Bowing Techniques for a Rich, Satisfying Sound** (ebook).

• **SINAI: The Desert & Bedouins of South Sinai's Central Regions.** Photos and text by Ruth Shilling. Published by Palm Press, Cairo, Egypt, 2003. Contains more than 100 full-color photos of the Sinai and the Bedouin people who live there. Available on Amazon.com.

*Flow of Well Being*, blog and Facebook page:

• flowofwellbeing.wordpress.com

• Facebook.com/flowofwellbeing

# ℑNDEX of 𝕋OPICS

## LEFT HAND

◆◆◆◆◆◆◆◆◆◆◆◆◆◆◆◆◆◆◆◆◆◆◆◆◆◆◆◆◆◆◆◆◆◆

CPSIA information can be obtained at www.ICGtesting.com
Printed in the USA
LVOW10s1759300316

481440LV00020B/755/P